Hit or Miss Management

OUR FOUNDER

HIT OR MISS
MANAGEMENT

Hit or Miss Management

The world's first organic, natural, holistic, environmentally sound management technique.

Gene Perret

Illustrated by Jeffrey Lieppman

J. P. Tarcher, Inc.
Los Angeles

Distributed by
Houghton Mifflin Company
Boston

**Library of Congress
Cataloging in Publication Data**

Perret, Gene.
Hit or miss management.

1. Management–Anecdotes, facetiae, satire,
etc. I. Title.
HD38.P426   658'.00207   79-91762
ISBN 087477-123-4

Design by John Brogna/Cynthia Eyring

Manufactured in the United States of America
Published by J. P. Tarcher, Inc.
9110 Sunset Blvd., Los Angeles, Calif. 90069

10   9   8   7   6   5   4   3   2   1
First Edition

To my dad, who permitted me to
inherit some of his wonderful sense of humor.

To my mom, who had the patience to
put up with both of us.

Contents

Acknowledgments

To my kids, Joey, Terry, Carole, and Linda, who did the bulk of the transcribing and typing and who ran the errands that I was too lazy to do myself.

There are a few more acknowledgments at the end of the book, but don't read them until you're finished. That's why they're at the end.

Nothing being more important than anything else, a man of knowledge chooses any act, and acts it out as if it mattered to him. His controlled folly makes him say that what he does matters and makes him act as if it did, and yet he knows that it doesn't so when he fulfills his acts he retreats in peace, and whether his acts were good or bad, or worked or didn't, is in no way any part of his concern.

Carlos Castaneda
A Separate Reality: Further
Conversations with Don Juan

Consider the lilies of the field, how they grow: They toil not, neither do they spin.

Matthew 6:28

Management is easy.

Gene Perret,
at a party one night.

Your author, guide, mentor, and host

Since we are going to be spending quite a few pages together, and since I am unquestionably going to be the leader and the shaper of your executive destiny with my innovative and astoundingly brilliant new hit or miss management theories, perhaps you should get to know me better.

Naturally, I will not print my full résumé; that document is more extensive than this book itself, since I average over nine jobs each fiscal year. (Isn't it nice to be so much in demand?)[1]

Nor will I print merely the highlights because with a career as glorious as mine, even the highlights could fill a volume.

I will list only the most salient and radiant accomplishments that have so copiously peppered my career.

I began my business career as a lowly apprentice for the Foremost Electric Company. The schedule called for graduation from apprenticeship after three and a half years. I completed it in three months.[2]

In order not to embarrass the other less talented apprentices, I moved to the rival, Eastern Electric Company, where I devised a computer-generated wiring procedure for electrical safety equipment. Unfortunately, the system was too advanced to become widely accepted by this rather backward industry. It was tried once and abandoned.[3]

I discarded my technical dalliance to become a leader of men, obtaining a position as manager of union relations

15

with McMonagle Enterprises, Inc., of Philadelphia. There I astounded the business world by negotiating a contract that revolutionized labor-management relations.[4]

Enjoying my work with people so immensely and recognizing how gifted I was at it, I expanded to become vice-president of public relations for Rhodus and Company of Seattle. My success here was so overwhelming that it became my longest single term of employment. The people of the community would not let me go.[5]

Having reached the pinnacle of public relations, I entered an even more challenging field. I introduced my ingenuity into accounting, a world that is replete with a creativity of its own. Again dissatisfied with archaic practices, I interjected my own creations and made a new name for myself.[6]

Deciding that my originality was too magnificent to be harnessed by the traditions of established firms, I became president of various new companies: Knechtel Products, Inc.,[7] Blaylock Mining Company,[8] Bagley Baking Company,[9] Robert Mills Enterprises,[10] and many, many others.[11]

Over the last several years, I have devoted my talents and skills to the business world at large.[12] My motivational speeches have roused many a lackadaisical worker into action,[13] and I have formulated the principles contained in *Hit or Miss Management*.

It must be apparent by now that my background is both extensive and varied and that I have never been content with effete procedures that are standard in most business establishments. Indeed, after reading my condensed résumé you can probably guess that my motto has always been "Mr. Perret thinks a lot."[14]

Editor's Notes

1. Isn't it questionable to be terminated so often?
2. The use of the word *completed* is misleading here. The record shows he was called into the apprentice supervisor's office and was told he "was finished."
3. It was plugged in the day of the New York blackout.
4. Philadelphia newspaper clippings reveal that the McMonagle Enterprises, Inc., building was burned to the ground in the workers' riot of 1956.
5. Seattle newspaper accounts indicate that angry residents of the suburb where Rhodus and Company was situated stormed the office building and held Mr. Perret hostage. Negotiations dragged on because the company had no interest in paying the ransom. The FBI was called in but refused to enter any transactions of less than five dollars.
6. Court records reveal that new name was No. 560551 in the county correctional institution.
7. Bankrupt (1964).
8. Receivership (1965).
9. Simply misplaced (196?).
10. Moved and left no forwarding address (1967).
11. All now either defunct or deformed.
12. No one will have him.
13. The word *action* should read *riot*.
14. Mr. Perret also "lies a lot."

CHAPTER 1

Management ignorance

or
How executives have been led astray by
the voluminous prevarications of Drucker,
McGregor, and others of their ilk, and
could have learned more from Captain
Walter Fargell and a bucket of fish.

Friends, I've always been a hole plugger. Whenever I see
vast holes of knowledge, I'm compelled to plug them.
Today I mount my trusty steed, Typewriter, and prepare to
attack management—well, perhaps not management so
much as the managerial-education system. Management
knowledge, taken as a whole, is a hole. I and my *Hit or Miss
Management* system are here to plug it.

Common sense suggests to us that the upper rungs of the
executive ladder would be inhabited by the more intelligent of those in the available work force; yet that's the exact
opposite of the conclusion anyone who has ever worked for
anyone else will draw. In varying degrees of eloquence,
they will all say, basically, "My boss is a nitwit." We have a
labor force of some 200 million workers. Can that many
people be wrong?

It distresses me to introduce myself to the reader on such

a polemic note. No doubt you managers out there in Bookland will dispute my argument and rush to your own and your compeers' defense. And although I find your loyalty commendable, I must point out to you that, seen in a larger context, your indignation is really only a surge of reflex parochialism. It is beneath you to take such a limited view when the real truth—about you and your business—is about to be spread out before you and offered as a feast of insights, observations, and damn clever comments.

Hit or Miss Management is a humanitarian work, but author and reader must be honest with each other if any benefit is to be realized.

Looking at things cool-headedly, we both must admit that we all know fellow swivel-chair jockeys and briefcase bearers who are relatively low on the I.Q. totem pole. Upper-level executives are not always the crème de la crème that the establishment would have us believe they are. Why is this? I'll tell you, but first a little lesson from nature—the first of many in this book.

If we look at a flock of sheep and one ram stands out as leader, we can safely assume that he is the strongest of the males. When he was challenged by all the other aspirants for the job of chief ram, he lowered his head and butted them all into submission, thus proving himself the worthiest of the flock. Not so in the managerial world, however. Here the leaders aren't selected by a natural process; they are picked and educated for the role by their superiors. When the selector is weak, the selectee is generally weaker still, and this weakness intensifies through the years. If rams had gone through this same selective process, today they'd all be falling off mountains.

Here's another example, this one from our friends in the ocean. Capt. Walter Fargell, a noted marine specialist, claims that he can take any seal from the open seas and train her to play the national anthem on a set of horns within about three hours. Now granted, that seal is never going to make it to the New York Philharmonic, and she doesn't perform the melody for the enjoyment of music but for the herring or halibut she gets as a reward. Nevertheless, she learns her task in three hours. In a series of remarkable tests conducted by the Wharton School of Business in Grand Junction, Colorado, it took a selected group of managers fourteen hours, three lunches, four canceled meetings, one feasibility study, and several phone calls among their secretaries just to learn to catch the fish in their mouths.

Perhaps it's unfair to compare animals and executives—it's like comparing oranges and nuts. Animals can do certain things that managers can't, and managers can do some things that animals can't. For example, because he doesn't have to, an executive doesn't learn to store his nuts for the winter, although many of us have had that suggested to us.

So let's look at the intelligence of some executives as compared to that of other Homo sapiens. To acquire some reading of their natural I.Q., examine that unique business phenomenon, the convention. Conventions are held at all times of the year and throughout every part of the world. At every moment of every day, some executives are sitting down to a seminar where they are given a little pad with a printing company's logo on it and handed a ball-point pen imprinted with the name of a bank. (Incidentally, that's further proof of the imbecility of some of those in management. Banks hand out 800 million ball-point pens a year, yet in their own establishments they have pens that don't work—*and* they chain them to the counters!) But let's get back to the business convention. Employees travel hundreds, even thousands of miles to attend these gatherings, and all at company expense. All of their meals are paid for through expense accounts, the rooms are provided by the company, much merrymaking and profuse drinking take place, there is always more than ample free time, and yet most of the upper-echelon executives bring their spouses. How smart can they be? It wouldn't take a seal three hours to learn that that's not the smartest thing to do.

Is my attack on managerial intelligence gratuitous? Definitely not. I've worked for too many of them and seen too much denseness on their parts. My career is full of stories of superior dumbness. Recounting them all would only serve to strain your patience—not to mention my credibility—but let me relate just one as a typical example.

Once we were having a company celebration for either a twenty-fifth-anniversary party or a retirement (I forget the specifics). This kind of affair was usually quite a popular social event at this particular plant. The employees would chip in so much for a meal, and part of the ticket price would go toward buying a nice gift for the honoree. The affair was held at a restaurant in the vicinity and after the formal celebration there was a bit of ad-lib drinking and backroom socializing. These were always late-night affairs, and the ones who went to them could be spotted the next day by their tired, bloodshot eyes and penchant for walking into walls.

After this memorable celebration, the late-nighters were milling about in the parking area. Our big management honcho kept asking people to help him find his car. He was a bit under the alcoholic weather, and the car was not his but borrowed from his brother-in-law. If *he* didn't know which car it was, we certainly didn't. We all told him that he had no option but to wait until everyone had left; the last car remaining would be his. Again, a trained seal could have figured that out quicker.

I was among the last to leave, and several of us talked to the manager and then went out to the parking lot to our various cars. As we climbed into them, we all noticed that only one car remained empty, our manager's car—the VW with the canoe tied to the top.

Oh, I know that's a hard story to believe, but there are even more incredible ones coming up, so you'd better get used to it.

It seems unbelievable because our society tends to think that the higher a person goes in the business world, the smarter he or she is. This is simply not axiomatic. It may not even be hypothetical.

None of this is related here to demean those executives. *Hit or Miss Management* intends not to censure these clowns but to convert them. As we shall see, bad management isn't the managers' fault; it's the system and, more accurately, the management theory and technique with which managers have been brought up that are the true culprits.

Somewhere in its history management has gone terribly wrong. *Hit or Miss Management* will show you where and tell you exactly who is responsible.

A Theory of Management Evolution

The first question any group who is lost will ask is "How did we get here?" Back to that superior example given— nature.

If you see a flock of sheep on a hillside and the leader is knock-kneed and cross-eyed, has a beer belly and only one limp horn hanging down over his ear and instead of standing tall and majestic he kind of leans against a rock all the time . . . you just have to ask yourself, "How did that s.o.b. get to be the leader?"

Well, as I pointed out so very clearly earlier, you'll never see that, but if you did I can guarantee that when the time comes for this ram to choose his successor, he is not going to select some young, vigorous, clear-eyed, well-muscled, sober stud. He's going to appoint a poor beast who is more knock-kneed, cross-eyed, and limp horned than he is. And when this unfortunate, four-legged creature ambles to the front of the herd and takes his leadership stance leaning against a rock, should we ridicule the beast or condemn the system that put him there in the first place?

The problem is one of education. As errors crept into management, they were perpetuated by being incorporated into the fund of managerial knowledge. It's as if one day a knock-kneed ram accidentally outbutted all of the opposition and then had the power to declare that henceforth all contenders for the head of the herd must come from the knock-kneed school of leadership. Then, from that group, a cross-eyed animal happened to walk away with the championship and issued a parallel proclamation. Well, you can foresee the results. Indeed in business you see them every day.

Sure, there are others who would claim to lead you out of the desert. Management Moseses with their commandments handed down from some unseen, all-knowing source. In the animal kingdom this doesn't happen. Nature quickly corrects an occasional accident, but in the executive world it becomes policy, and there's no one around with the experience and guts to cry "Halt!" but me.

I've read Peter Drucker's *Managing for Results* because at one point in my callow youth I wanted to get results when I managed, and I found his book on a sale table for fifty-nine cents. (I should have taken the hint.) I've perused Townsend's *Up the Organization* because at times I've wanted to up the organization. I've studied McGregor's *The Human Side of Enterprise* because I am forced to deal with humans. And I've read the *Peter Principle* because . . . well, frankly, I read that one because I thought it was dirty, but none of these books accomplishes a thing or educates one iota. They simply perpetuate the errors of management by giving them scholarly credence. (For example, ask yourself this about McGregor's X and Y theories: How dependable can a formula be if its own creator refuses to give it a name?) These books are equivalent to an academic treatise that might be entitled *Why the Knock-Kneed Ram Is Most Proficient for Leadership in Mountainous Terrain, Especially When Coupled with Nearsightedness and Enhanced by a Horn That Lacks Rigidity.*

"Why is this?" you ask.

"Good question," I respond.

Two phenomena have collided to produce this woeful state of managerial-education information.

The First Law of Management Dynamics

Management flows in an upward current. Most upper-level executives come up through the ranks. As they progress they cause an updraft and leave a vacuum behind them. When a new employee is sucked into that vacuum he often reports to the person who just vacated that same position.

Now it doesn't always happen that cleanly, but, for the most part, when you are appointed to a position, the person you are reporting to has served in that same position or in a similar one. He knows the ropes. He has been there.

Naturally, the outgoing employee wants the incoming employee to work harder than he worked because now his underling's hard work will make him look better in his superior's eyes.

When he was in the job he learned how to take all the shortcuts possible. Now, when an underling comes in, he naturally wants that new employee to work as hard as possible, so he fabricates reasons for not taking advantage of some of the goldbricking opportunities inherent in the position—the same goldbricking opportunities that this man himself may have created.

This particular phenomenon has gone on since the invention of the hierarchical system. How can one describe this law definitely? What is the $E = mc^2$ of it? Don't ask me, I'm into collecting matchbooks, not physics. "And what is the result of this ongoing practice?" you ask. Good lord, I've laid all the empirical data in front of you, must I draw the conclusions, too? All right, I'll do it this time, but I'm not going to spend the entire book playing Sherlock Holmes to your Dr. Watson.

The conclusion is that by disallowing the shortcuts,

upper management has become the champion of inefficiency.

Drawing from nature again: we often see ants carrying
food back to their colony for the benefit of all the colonists.
Theorize how long an ant community would survive if each
food bearer had to write a report on how much food she
bore, had to go to meetings to tell how she was going to
carry more food the next month, and so on.

Now frankly, aren't you sorry you didn't think of those
things yourself instead of asking me?

The Second Law of Management Dynamics

Everyone is familiar with this phenomenon and with a
little examination of conscience will have to admit to being
a transgressor sometimes.

Someone tells you a story about a third party that amuses
you. The story just begs to be repeated. You recount it to
several acquaintances. Then, on one occasion, when the
story for one reason or another needs a little lift, you add a
bit of dramatic intensity. You make the story just a little bit
better than the original. Intuitively you know that the story
would have been funnier if this had happened, and so you
add it.

Then later, when the enhanced story is repeated again,
you add, "You should have seen the look on his face." You
now are a participant.

The next time you tell it, it might possibly be about *you*.

After years and years of recounting the story and adding
to it, you yourself begin to *believe* the fabrications.

This has happened with managerial data. The myths
have been passed on for so long that people now give credibility to them, and all they are really good for is a big laugh.
We forgot why we were telling the story and began to act
on it.

As a consequence of this phenomenon, all of the "real"
information available to executives is based on myth. The

books that are printed about management are, without exception, very learned treatises dealing with prevarication. Lies. Falsehoods.

All of us in the executive community today are a gaggle of confused rodents following after a cluster of inept pied pipers. Not one of these befuddled docents knows either how to play the flute or how to get to the river. And then they have the audacity to turn around and give us music and map-reading lessons.

That's why this book is so vital. It is an effort to return to the unclouded facts. It is a stripping away of the mythical old manager's tales that have become so widely accepted. *Hit or Miss Management* adamantly believes that all executive wisdom is contained between these covers.

This volume, and this volume alone, is the salvation for management today. I deeply regret that you had to pay to buy this book in a store. I would have preferred to appear to each of you in a burning bush and hand this information to you engraved on stone tablets.

CHAPTER 2

Why HOM is the right system

or

If nature were run with the same
efficiency as today's corporations,
only God could afford a tree.

Dear Reader and, I trust, Friend, we have known each other for just one chapter now, and I have already challenged a few long-held and cherished dogmas. I fully expect to be challenged in return.

You'd be remiss if you didn't say to me right now, "Okay, wise guy, after your high-falutin' first chapter, what makes your system so far superior to all the other management literature that I've read? Huh?" And I'd be irresponsible if I didn't answer your rudely stated interrogation.

Hit or miss management is the only feasible system because it returns to basics. It's the only natural, totally organic management program—the method that mimics nature. Remember we said previously that somewhere along the way management went wrong? Well, any attempt just to repair that would be mere patchwork. We'd really be mending a torn garment with cloth as faulty as the garment we're trying to fix. So my book transcends that approach. It journeys back to the era before the errors crept in. Since no one knows exactly when that was, let's go back to the very beginning.

Nature is the ideal management system. Certainly she is a better teacher than Drucker and McGregor and all of the other so-called scholars of the field. Why? Because nature has survived, while industry rumor has it that those guys are barely eking out a livelihood.

I can anticipate your rebuttals already. "Did dinosaurs survive?" you ask with a smirk. "And the dodo?" you shout from the back of the hall. Certainly not, but that was not so much the fault of poor management as it was the natural consequences of changing times. Blacksmiths are rare today, not because we were saddled with poor smithing, but because there is little demand for them.

So enough of your smart-ass questions. Let's move on to facts.

Nature not only has survived but has survived magnificently. All of its facets continue to prosper and flourish with none of the turmoil that surrounds the human business enterprise system for which Drucker, McGregor, and others of their ilk are responsible.

Has the cost of building a bird's nest risen dramatically in the past decade? Do you see gaily colored, winged creatures marching around in front of a tree, armed with sarcastically worded placards protesting that their nests are being converted to condominiums?

You've no doubt purchased, or at least seen, those ant farms that are sold as educational toys for children. Did you ever hear of anybody having to return one to the store because the ant community had been beleaguered with labor problems?

Have you ever seen an ant transporting a piece of food several times his size and weight being stopped and badgered by a shop steward because he was carrying too much?

Tell me of just one incident where a family of beavers

one if your business hasn't been doing that well) in your hot little hands.

The *Hit or Miss Management* system is the correct one simply because it is precisely what it says it is—hit or miss. It is natural. It is organic. Nature has operated glowingly for immeasurable years on a hit or miss basis. A single example should suffice.

An acorn does not hire a consulting firm to do a soil feasibility study at considerable cost before falling to the ground. It simply falls. If the elements are favorable, it germinates. If the elements are unsuitable, it turns into chemicals that feed those seeds that do take root. Does the system work? Have you ever seen an acorn in an unemployment line? Indeed, not only does the system work, but it is inexpensive. Oak trees don't go bankrupt any more than beavers do.

Effective management is that simple. All the hullabaloo that surrounds it is generated by greed or fear.

Let's take our same oak tree and transform it through the magic of the written word into Oak Tree, Inc. Now, instead of a simple, beautiful tree that only God can make, it is a business establishment that the New York Stock Exchange can make. Now it might operate like this.

ACT ONE

SETTING: Office of the chairman of the tree. The chairman sits in a large swivel leaf behind a handsomely carved oak (what else?) desk. He has gathered all his executive nuts together.

CHAIRMAN. Gentlenuts, I've just returned from the international convention of the OTMS (Oak Tree Management Society).

VICE-PRESIDENT NO 1. How was it, Chief?

CHAIRMAN. It was lousy. The food was rotten, the travel was

terrible. I don't know why they hold those things in Denver in the middle of winter. Frankly, gentlenuts, I was embarrassed there.

VICE-PRESIDENT NO 2. But Chief, you couldn't have been embarrassed . . .

CHAIRMAN. Shut up and listen, and you'll see why I was embarrassed.

VICE-PRESIDENT NO 2. Yessir.

(All heads lower to study the blank legal pads before them. Some nervous doodling goes on as the chairman continues.)

CHAIRMAN. At our Germination Council meeting, all of the directors turned in reports about their own trees. By comparison our performance was abominable.

Baser, what was our acorn production differential last year?

BASER. Sir, it was up 0.02 percent from the previous year and . . .

CHAIRMAN. *(angrily interrupting)* The international average increase was 0.0316.

BASER. But sir, several of our branches were hampered by dry rot and . . .

CHAIRMAN. *(ignoring his protestations and turning to another)* Tuttle, what was our germination rate?

TUTTLE. It was up from the previous year . . .

CHAIRMAN. *(barking angrily)* What was the rate?

TUTTLE. Twelve point forty-three percent, sir.

CHAIRMAN. Four and seven-tenths points off of the international average. Are you proud of that?

TUTTLE. No sir.

CHAIRMAN. Are any of you proud of that?

ALL NUTS IN UNISON. No sir.

VICE-PRESIDENT NO 1. *(bravely)* But we can't overlook the drought conditions that . . .

CHAIRMAN. *(banging his fist on the desk)* I don't want excuses, damn it, I want results.

(pregnant pause)

   We're supposed to be running a goddamn tree here.

(pregnant pause)

   Now I want to see an improvement immediately, or I'm going to have to do some pruning.

(He pauses to let that sink in.)

   We've got enough deadwood in this tree already. I want our production output at all levels and in all of your areas of responsibility to increase by a minimum of one-quarter of one percent per month, beginning immediately. Now get out of here.

(sounds of chairs scraping and papers rattling as we end the act)

ACT TWO

SETTING: *Branch manager's office. Her staff is gathered there.*

BRANCH MANAGER. I just came from the boss's office and he tore into me royally. I'm sick and tired of getting my shell cracked because you nuts aren't doing your job. And don't look around the room at each other, because I'm talking to all of you! Starting today, I want production to increase by one-half of one percent per month.

(mumbling heard around the room)

That's right, grumble and mumble, but, goddammit, get it done. Weiskopf, I want a full study on soil conditions done and on my desk by next Tuesday. Illes, I want to see a review of projected rainfall the same day.

WEISKOPF. But Boss, we don't have the people.

BRANCH MANAGER. Full staff works overtime.

ILLES. But Boss, we don't have the budget.

BRANCH MANAGER. I don't care how much this damn thing costs. Get those reports done and get that output moving upwards or all of you will be looking for another tree to hang around on.

ACT THREE

SETTING: Cellular structure of the tree. The foreman addresses those cells under him.

FOREMAN. You guys have been sitting on your duffs, and you got my ass in a sling. Well, the vacation is over. I'm not gonna lose my job because of a bunch of cellulose creeps. Either you get working eight goddamn hours a day, or I personally guarantee that I'll turn you into woodpecker fodder. Unnerstand?

The Oak Tree, Inc., example seems ludicrous, and it is. All management just takes itself too seriously. It's no big deal.

Drucker's *Management for Results* has a very deceptive title. All management gets results. The question is, Are they good results or bad results? I think that with Drucker's system you have a fifty-fifty chance of either one. You don't have a guarantee of good results, nor are you assured of bad results. So why take it that seriously? With the hit or miss system you have a fifty-fifty chance, too. If you hit, you get good results; if you miss, you get bad results. You're in the same boat, only this system is much less trouble to learn than Drucker's.

When it comes time for management to make decisions, the present practice is to form a committee to investigate which method to use, then to conduct a feasibility study, and then to bring in some people to perform cost accounting—how much is this going to cost, how much profit will it make, and so on. When you add up all the man-hours that go into this process, you begin to see that it costs hundreds of thousands of dollars to make a single decision. And after all this, when you finally implement the decision, either you're right or you're wrong. If you're right, you make the money you were going to make anyway. If you're wrong, you start over again, and it costs you more hundreds of thousands of dollars to jump through the hoops all over again.

With the hit or miss system, you don't do any studies at all. You simply make a decision. If it's right, you make the profit. If it's wrong, you haven't wasted all that money finding out if you were going to be right or not.

As is the case with government, the best management is no management at all. You hit or you miss. Somebody makes a decision. Anyone can do it. Either right or wrong. Either way it's no big deal, because if they are right that's groovy and if they are wrong that's life. We are all far too judgmental these days. Right, wrong. Who really knows? The guy who found a way to fit the engine into the trunk compartment of the Pinto was congratulated for getting things right. The person who figured out how to use asbestos lining to cut down the heat in hair dryers won an efficiency award. The kindly inventor of the exploding harpoon got a promotion. Right, wrong. Who's to say? And I think that's what you'll find the rest of this book is about.

Just take a look at management as it is practiced today. A company will spend a fortune trying to find executives who are going to make the right decisions. When it finds those executives and they make the right decisions, the company has to promote them. It has to give them a raise in order to keep them. When a firm hires executives who make the wrong decisions, it has to fire them and spend even more money to find executives who are going to make the right decisions. It's a very costly procedure, and, of course, the cost is transferred to the product the company manufactures.

When we learn to see decisions in the larger context, when we no longer place so much importance on whether the decisions are right or not, then we can keep the executives we've got. If they make a right decision, great, but we don't have to promote them. And by the same token, if they make a wrong decision, we don't have to fire them. It's much more economical and humane to use the hit or miss management system, and, as you'll see, it all comes out the same in the end anyway.

Since a wrong decision is as good as a right decision, the only error is no decision at all. Therefore, it's good management practice to get into the habit of making decisions even when there are no problems, because you'll find out as you gain more managerial experience that every time you make a decision, it creates a new problem anyway. But once you've made *your* decision, it becomes someone else's problem.

CHAPTER 3

Decision making

or
Making a decision is like going
to the dentist—once it's over you're
amazed at how painless it really was, and
most executives only do it twice a year.

Hit or Miss Management's advice on decision making is deceptively uncomplicated: Make the decision. It's no big deal. So just make your decision. All right, I can almost hear the cynics out there in Readerland saying to themselves, "I pay $8.95 for a book, and he tells me that when it's time to make a decision, make a decision?" Before you storm angrily back to the bookstore and punch that sweet bookseller in the nose, hear me out. Then if you still feel you want to punch the bookseller, be my guest.

All decisions are a gamble. They are a crapshoot no matter how you slice it, unless you happen to be a fortune-teller (and you see very few crystal balls at board meetings). Decision making is pure chance, like drawing to a thirteen in blackjack in Las Vegas. No matter how long it takes you to decide whether to take a hit, no matter how strenuously you agonize over your choices, you cannot change the card that is going to come up next. . . . You might as well make your choice—draw or stay—and let the chips fall where they may.

Picture members of big business sitting at a blackjack table. Before they take a card, they'll have to conduct a statistical analysis of the probability of going bust on a thirteen. They'll hire experts, have meetings, and finally draw up several long-winded reports. It will take so long that the other players at the table will leave and the dealer might even retire before the corporation finally decides to say, "Okay, hit me." When that card is turned up, though, it will be exactly the same as the vacationer's from Omaha who, without thinking, said, "Hit me." They will both either win or lose, but with one huge difference—the corporation, if it wins, will have expended all of its winnings in research.

The sharp reader may argue that in business decision making is much more complex than this and that there is a distinct difference between a decision and a good decision. I'll concede that, although, frankly, I'm getting tired of the reader constantly arguing with me. If you didn't want to come into contact with controversial ideas, why the hell didn't you read a novel? Yes, Smarty-pants, there *is* a difference between a decision and a good decision, but nobody knows that until the resolution has been implemented and the results evaluated. It's all hindsight.

Do research, study, and tormented meditation produce decisions of a distinctively high quality, as corporate powers contend? Certainly they do, but random selection has a higher batting average.

Based on statistics alone, the hit or miss procedure carries a fifty-fifty rate of success; and I maintain you'll be correct more often than that because in making snap judgments the intuitive faculties enter in. These hunches, feelings, suspicions, and gut reactions are always written out of feasibility studies and research reports, leaving the decision to rest solely on the analytic capacities of the decision makers. Friends, I rest my case.

The established system cannot better the hit or miss rate and more often than not falls short of it.

Ordinary people worry for months about whether they

should go into business for themselves. They consult their lawyers, their bankers, their accountants. They present proposals to investors; they revise their plans again and again, refining each element to perfection. How successful are they? Statistics show that better than 80 percent of new businesses fail.

Even people sitting in a high-class restaurant deliberate at length over which dish to order, and more often than not they make a bad choice; yet lions, using my system, spring at the first zebra they see and very rarely get one that isn't tasty.

Do present-day decision-making procedures come up with anything nearly as delicious? Let's study the following case history.

Case History No. 42757

(Note: The name of this company has been changed to protect the imbecilic.) When Bliveden Motors was designing its luxury car, the Bliveden Bat, there arose a serious engineering controversy over the placement of the clock on the dashboard.

Hundreds of thousands of dollars' worth of research had already unequivocally determined that the clock should be digital. Now, however, there were two schools of thought regarding the clock's location. One engineering team felt the clock should be positioned on the left side of the dashboard so that drivers could glance at it as they checked the rear-view mirror. Obviously, many drivers are anxious to know the exact time at which cars are approaching them in the passing lane.

The rival engineering group contended just as vehemently that the clock should be in the center of the dashboard so that the passengers could see it as well. I suppose the logic here is, Why would anyone ride with a driver who wouldn't even give him the time of day?

Those in upper management, predictably, saw the sense

in both arguments and so were forced to "make the deci
sion." At considerable cost, they immediately hired a consulting firm. When the firm's ambivalent results were in,
they had to hire a new team of engineers to study the am-
biguity of the report. Other departments were asked to
participate in the debate and give their opinions.

Ultimately, the clock was placed in the center of the
dashboard. "Why?" you ask. Reader, you disappoint me.
You should know by now that there was no rationale behind
this decision; it's simply that the center-clockers were more
powerful debaters than the left-hand-clockers.

Was it a correct decision? Only time will tell. But either
way, the cost of each car rose several thousand dollars.

As a buyer, I don't want to purchase a car for $12,000 just
so the person who's bumming a ride can see what time it is.
I'd rather pay $4,000, screw the clock, and buy my pas-
sengers a watch.

End of Case History.

End of argument.

The ears on my typewriter are burning because it can
hear so many of you skeptics proclaiming, "Perret won't tell
us how to solve problems because he probably doesn't
know how." No doubt you're the same readers who claim
that Freud proposed his theories on dreams because he
could never stay awake.

Certainly I can teach you the mechanics of arriving at a
solution—and I think I will, just to confound my critics—
but remember that I neither advise nor condone them. In
fact, I believe that this process is so easy to learn that my
explanation is only wasting paper and printer's ink. However, you're paying for the book. I got my copy free.

There are three basic steps to making a decision: (1) define the problem; (2) gather the correct facts; and (3) make
your choice. Realize, however, that the numbers in front of
those steps glorify them far beyond their worth. They are
not as difficult as they sound. You go through them when
you're putting on your socks in the morning. Infants do it

when they decide whether to throw their strained peas on the floor or on their father. But to clarify, I'll pose a hypothetical problem and solve it through these three steps.

Let's say you want to go to grandmother's house. First you define the problem. Where does grandmother live? Over the hill. Wasn't that easy? And top executives want to get paid big money for doing this all day.

Now you have to gather the correct facts. It doesn't take an I.Q. of 165 to figure out that a road map might help here. You have to have the correct map, though. If grandmom lives over the hill in Hollywood, you want a map of Hollywood, California, not Hollywood, Florida, unless your grandmother lives in Florida, in which case you're okay.

But suppose you check the correct map, get to the address she gave you, and then find an amusement park situated there. Had you checked more thoroughly you would have learned that your grandmom is senile and forgot that she moved to Leisure World four years ago. You have to check your data, and you have to keep in closer touch with your nanny.

Was any of the preceding so very difficult? No. Was it that astounding? Of course not. Remember, though, that I told you about that earlier. Don't blame me for wasting your time when you're the ones who forced me into it.

What you've just seen is a simple solution of a problem that anyone with an I.Q. of 65 could have solved, including your author. But if you had asked any major corporation in America to drive you to your grandmother's house, you'd still be sitting on your ass in your living room with your overcoat on. Why? Because management can't make simple decisions.

Oh, sure, all executives boast of having decision-making skills, but what they really do is pass the decisions on to other people. At last we find out what they're really good at—avoiding making decisions.

If decision making is as easy as I say and as all open-minded people will agree that it is, then why, traditionally, does management pass it along? Why do executives display those plaques on their desks that read, "The buck stops here?" Because they know that every decision is a crap-shoot, a gamble. They don't like those fifty-fifty odds, so they delegate it to an underling. If, in hindsight, the underling's conclusion turns out to be the right one, the superior will accept the copious accolades. Should it be erroneous, however, he'll be fierce in his blame.

Therefore, until the entire world is converted to hit or miss management, I advise you to play the self-protective establishment game. Make no determination and push the problem further down the corporate ladder. This is fairly simple to do; after all, your superiors aren't going to push you for an answer because they don't want to have to give an answer themselves.

You can (1) delay your decision, claiming the need for more time for research; (2) turn the problem over to another department for more information; (3) find a precedent and give that as your decision (then you'll have a predecessor to blame); or (4) never give any answer, and the problem may go away.

Allow me to cite my own ingenuity in creative procrastination.

Case History No. 73501

My superiors posed a sticky problem to me once: "Should we use a hex nut on this size bolt in this particular operation or a wing nut?" They left the solution entirely in my capable hands. I could have applied the three decision-making principles, but why bother? Why the hell should I stick my neck out? If the company folded because I advocated wing nuts instead of hex nuts, that's a black mark on my record. Instead, I immediately called for a cost evaluation of the problem. In so doing, I transferred the dilemma onto the shoulders of another manager in another department.

Of course, I realized I merely transferred this to another manager who was also adept at delaying. He said, "I can't have an answer for you for at least six months." Publicly I ranted and raved but privately I wanted to write that manager a thank-you note.

Eight months later the report came back. It took an extra two months because the manager of the accounting department "decided" that other problems would take priority over mine. Nevertheless, the report was now on my desk. It was long and complicated, and it said nothing.

This was an accomplished manager, adept at avoiding all decision making. The report was saturated with ambiguities and devoid of conclusions. The hex nut might be best in certain circumstances, it said, but in others the wing nut is preferred, etc., etc. The decision was still squatting firmly on my shoulders.

I fully expected this, but at least I had had my eight-month vacation. Now the decision had to be made, so I took firm action. I appointed a committee.

Now, a committee is to decision making what a pin strategically placed in the back of a frog's head is to the frog—totally paralyzing.

The committee is ubiquitous in management. Nothing is done without one, and with one, nothing ever gets done.

But I will say this: once a committee had been created, decisions followed with the quickness of raindrops in a monsoon. They decided who should chair the committee. When would the meetings be held? Where would the sessions take place? Who would take the minutes? They labored over what the committee would be called. The Hex Nut/Wing Nut Study Committee was eliminated because the fact that the hex nut was given top billing seemed to imply that it would be favored. The appellation Nut Study Committee was considered at several meetings but eventually dropped.

You will notice that these were all very weighty decisions on which much time was spent. You will also notice that the net effect was to postpone making the decision on whether to use hex or wing nuts.

And, of course, any committee always has available the ultimate in delaying tactics: they can form their own sub-committee(s). We previously saw that the choosing of a name for this group posed some difficulty; we "decided" to form a committee within the committee to come up with suggestions for a name for the original committee. As you can see, this could well go on ad infinitum because the committee within the committee also needs a name, which they would have to decide on before they could attack the pressing problem of naming the original committee. We never did get a name for our committee because the problem went away, as you'll see.

While all this was going on, the factory workers pragmatically solved the problem themselves, and they did it in true *Hit or Miss Management* style. One shouted to the other, "Hey, should we use a [expletive deleted] hex nut on this [expletive deleted] bolt, or a [expletive deleted] wing nut?"

Another answered, "Let's use the [expletive deleted] wing nut."

The first one queried, "Don't they cost a [expletive deleted]-load more?"

The other worker explained, "[expletive deleted] that. The wing nut's faster, and we can get the [expletive deleted] out of here and go get a beer."

"That's A-[expletive deleted]-okay with me," the first agreed.

They solved the problem with no fanfare and no committees and no cost evaluations and no baloney. Why? Because they were just nuts-and-bolts kind of guys and not "decision makers."

End of Case History.

CHAPTER 4

Plain facts about management

or

A manager's first duty is to
himself. If you're the low man on the
totem pole, you won't get much help
from the wooden heads above you.

I hope that by now the majority of you see the wisdom of
Hit or Miss Management and are willing to subscribe to its
precepts. Welcome aboard!

However, the author must admit to being faced with a
dichotomy at this point. This is a how-to book for the working
executive. We proclaim *Hit or Miss Management* to be
the only natural management system and hope that all of
our readers will heartily subscribe to its doctrine, yet we
must concede that most present-day programs are not
based on the *Hit or Miss Management* precepts.

Therefore, henceforth our purpose must be twofold:
first, to foster and explain the precepts of *Hit or Miss Management*; and second, to instruct our readers in how to
cope, survive, and prosper under the existing, inept management processes.

It's not an undemanding task, but read on. Your author is
damned clever.

Management's First Responsibility

What is the manager's first responsibility? Peter Drucker tells us that the manager's first responsibility should always derive from the goals of the business enterprise. The objectives of every manager should spell out his or her contribution to the attainment of company goals in all areas of the business. Anything else, he admonishes, is shortsighted and impractical.

I say, go to a farm and watch a bull eating hay. He will relish it, and then it will go through his alimentary canal, and the nourishment will be biologically drawn out to keep the bull strong and functioning. Whatever isn't used by the bull is deposited to replenish the earth with minerals. That deposit is what Drucker's statements amount to.

Hit or Miss Management says the manager's first responsibility is to get a raise and/or a promotion (which I will henceforth refer to as R/P).

Very simply stated, that's why you show up each morning. It's your reason for unsnapping your briefcase. You're there to get ahead. This is not a condemnation of executives; it's purely a statement of fact.

The opposite is also true. The corporation exists to make a profit for itself and not to further the wealth of its executives. Here is a tragedy on a grand scale. The apparent oneness of an executive and his company is, in fact, an ineluctable (go ahead, look it up—I'll wait) duality.

The executive is not a corporation. He is not a soulless conglomeration of books and financial reports with nothing more on his mind than dividends and tax loopholes. He is a living creature with conscience and emotions. He may say he is devoted to the company in order to arouse enough strength to respond to the alarm clock at 6:30 each morning, but don't you believe it. All he is devoted to is himself, and there is nothing wrong with that.

Devotion is a deeply ingrained emotion. Young children are devoted to becoming movie stars or athletes, explorers or pilots when they grow up. You never hear a youngster say, "When I grow up I want to work for Amalgamated Aluminum." Very few kids have pictures of executives hanging in their bedrooms. Inspect the walls of 100 youngsters' bedrooms, and you won't find a single General Motors pennant. Children don't stand outside business offices to get the autographs of the non-hourly-wage employees as they leave the building.

Youngsters don't change as they grow up. They simply become more realistic. Deep down inside, all of us still want to be football players or ballet dancers, but gradually we realize that we're not fast enough, or strong enough, or skillful enough. So we must face the cruel fact that we do have to make a living. That's when we sit down for the job interview with Amalgamated Aluminum.

This is not devotion, it's desperation. If Amalgamated Aluminum doesn't offer the salary we think we can demand, then we walk down the street to Consolidated Aluminum. You'd really have to stretch your dictionary to make that a definition of devotion.

Why are we sitting there answering the demeaning questions of the smug interviewer of Consolidated Aluminum? Because we feel called by God to save the aluminum industry? No, because we want to make a buck. Not even just a buck, but a few more bucks than Amalgamated was willing to pay.

How about after you get the job? Then aren't the executives devoted to the company? Do you think the smug interviewer is there to search out the anointed one who will be the new Moses of aluminum? He's there because that's where his paycheck will be on Friday.

Certainly he wants to select the very best candidate for the job opening. Why? Not out of love for aluminum, but because that will impress his boss. And his boss will be delighted because it will help her, in turn, influence her boss. If the chain continues, the interviewer may even move up another rung on the corporate ladder and find that his Friday paycheck is a bit larger than before.

That, my friends, is what management is all about. It's the domino theory in reverse. You try to get all the dominos to stand up through a chain reaction.

It's so important that we should state this clearly. The purpose of management, from the lowliest to the most august position, is to do a job that impresses your boss. Your superior will then use your good work to increase his favor with his boss, and so on up the ladder. Everyone keeps this fragile chain unbroken because at the end of it is dangling the reward—moola.

This is nature's way. Everyone who has ever owned a cat has told the story of how once that feline proudly displayed himself to his owner with dead prey in his mouth. He was doing the natural, organic thing: trying to impress his "boss."

Ask yourself this: Did the cat feel that that unfortunate little animal *had* to be captured and dispatched? Was a harmless bird or a small rodent a threat to the safety of the household? Of course not, and you can bet the cat knew that. He was merely hoping that by showing his prowess as a hunter, he would receive a reward—perhaps a bit of extra food in his bowl that evening.

There is nothing to be ashamed of when we do the same as that cat. Indeed, it's reason to be proud. This type of activity is the very backbone of the free-enterprise system.

Management is *all* facade. Take away an executive's office building, carpeted inner office, huge desk, oversized leather chair, and the diplomas hanging on the walls, take away the business attire and the briefcase, and what have you got? A person standing in the middle of a vacant lot holding a stack of business cards because there's no place left to put them.

CHAPTER 5

Meetings

or
The executives' two favorite
pastimes combined into one—wasting hours
and keeping minutes.

In a fascinating series of experiments conducted by Dr. Wilhelm Richmond at Feldman University, executives from all branches of industry, business, and government were placed in a maze. (Dr. Richmond's brilliance can be seen in the way he cut out the middle man. Instead of using rats for the experimentation and then applying the data to human beings, he experimented directly on managers.) These executives, who were at various levels on the corporate ladder and from different geographical locations, represented a typical cross section of the managerial world.

Various enticements were placed at the end of the maze in order to see how quickly the executives would memorize the complicated corridors and arrive at their reward. The enticements were the old executive standbys—midday cocktails, expense-account privileges, cash bonuses, washroom keys, and the like.

Without going into more detail than you'd want to know, I can tell you that Dr. Richmond's experiments proved conclusively that the quickest way to get the manager to learn the tortuous route was to send him a notice that a meeting was being held at the end of the maze.

Hit or Miss Management contends that meetings are un-natural, inorganic, and accomplish nothing. Lions have been the kings of the jungle for years, but never once have they held a meeting to insure the continuance of their dynasty. Nor has a beaver ever chewed down a tree and then gnawed a gavel from the lumber. Beavers don't need gavels because they don't need Robert's rules of order be-cause they don't need meetings.

Managers love meetings. Because of this love affair, the meeting has become virtually the most vital organ of the economic system. It is the heart muscle that pumps the life-giving plasma to all branches of business and industry. When executives retreat into a paneled room with a pol-ished table, that room is transformed into a ventricle. The decisions these men and women make are the contrac-tions that force the vital fluid through the veins and the arteries of our businesses. In fact, for many managers, meetings are a sexual experience. They love them with an orgasmic fervor.

Why do executives love these assemblies so much? For many managers, meetings are like a return to the womb. If they need to feel comfortable, protected, sheltered, and separated from the outside world, what better sanctuary have they than the meeting?

Behind the closed doors of the executive session, the manager is impervious to the attacks of his natural pred-ator, the people under him. Surely you, at some time, have tried to see a so-called superior, only to be told by his sec-retary that "Mr. So-and-so is in a meeting." Translated into the vernacular, this means that Mr. So-and-so is in his for-tress. It cannot be penetrated by arrow, brick, burning oil, mortar fire, rocket, laser beam, or shop steward. He cannot be reached by phone, messenger, telegram, smoke signal, mental telepathy, or sky writer. He cannot be called from the meeting for any reason short of a death in the family, and even then only if it is his own.

"The boss is in a meeting" is an invincible defense. Watch a hawk chasing a rabbit sometime. The predator will change direction each time the rabbit does and relentlessly wait for a chance to swoop down and snatch up that prey. Once the rabbit retreats into a hole, though, the hawk will fly away looking for another meal. This bird doesn't go to the rabbit's secretary and say, "What's the rabbit doing in there, and was that an important hole?" It's useless. The smart manager trains subordinates so that they react the same way.

Another reason that executives have grown attached to the meeting is because it is a status symbol. They have meetings to go to, while the common worker doesn't. There's never been a worker who had to go to a meeting— the executives would never permit it. And even if they do go to something that resembles a meeting, the executives have given it a different name: a discussion, a bull session, a get-together, or some other such appellation that is completely devoid of status.

Meetings are clearly reserved for the mighty. Listen the next time your boss comes out and announces, "If anyone needs me, I'll be at a meeting." It almost sounds like it should be followed by a sing-songy "naa naa na-naa naa."

A particularly noteworthy depravity is the luncheon meeting. Executives can't give up their addiction even while taking care of natural bodily functions. The next step is to have the booths in the executive washroom arranged in a neat circle with a legal pad and ball-point pen conspicuously present in each one.

Meetings are probably the biggest cause of inefficiency in business today. While our economy suffers, executives steadfastly cling to their meetings and won't admit that they are pandering to their own baser instincts, proclaiming instead that they are actually solving our economic woes. While declaring their devotion to economic stability, they continue to hold all those meetings that, in effect, are stopping the growth of business. It's like taking the wheels off your car to figure out how to make it go faster.

As a *Hit or Miss Management* executive, you are going to have to attend and even hold some meetings; it's too firmly entrenched a tradition to be uprooted. However, that doesn't mean you can't make the most of it. After all, if you want to buy a puppy, you are going to have to clean the rugs every now and then. And I believe if you could chemically analyze what goes on at meetings, it would turn out to be the same as the stuff you're cleaning off the rugs.

Meetings Where You Are One of the Indians

If you are one of the Indians, there is very little you can do to control the meeting. Your main function is to try to appear knowledgeable.

Keep in mind our axiom that nothing worthwhile is ever accomplished at meetings. They are held strictly for the gratification of the executives. The most you can hope to achieve is a good grade for yourself with the bigwigs. The following are various ways to accomplish this.

The Adroit Use of the Nod

Never speak at a meeting unless you have to. A good rule to remember is that it is better to remain silent and be thought a fool than to speak up and remove all doubt.

The nod, however, can be a very powerful offensive weapon. You simply wait until somebody says something profound, then you nod. If the bosses like it, you become associated with it by your nod. And if they don't, you can adroitly transform the nod into part of a massage movement for a sore neck. In fact, I knew one gentleman who had worked all the way up to the position of executive vice-president before his wisdom was correctly diagnosed as Saint Vitus's dance.

Looking Intelligent

During meetings, try to look as if you know what's going on. I managed to develop this skill to its highest degree, training myself to sleep with a furrowed brow and a pensive look on my face so that I could nap while appearing to be deep in intelligent thought. If you try this and want to cover yourself, tell your coworkers that you always breathe deeply when you're getting near the solution of a problem. If you happen to start snoring, they'll all think the problem is almost solved.

Another way to appear intelligent is to suck on something, such as the end of a pencil, the earpiece of your eyeglasses, or almost anything else that isn't attached to your or anyone else's body, with the possible exception of doorknobs. Why sucking on things is a sign of intellectual activity, however, is the subject of a whole other volume.

Controlling the Conversation

At meetings, silence is golden. If you must speak, keep the conversation away from business. Swing the discussion around to something on which you're well versed. A perfect ploy is to direct the topic to a book that you've just read. I always had a lot of success with statements such as the following: "Boy, is this a tough problem. We're going to have to get some real good horses to work on this one. Some horses that are as strong and courageous as, say, Black Beauty." Or, "This problem that we're trying to solve is really a mystery, isn't it? It's like trying to figure out whether Huckleberry Finn really killed his father or not." Or even, "Boy, this one is a real mystery. You know who we could use to solve this? The Hardy Boys."

You'll notice the very clever and facile way that I guided the conversation toward a topic on which I could easily converse. It will work for you, too.

Meetings Where You're the Chief

You yourself will conduct meetings. Until the industrial world is converted to the *Hit or Miss Management* system, meetings will remain a constant thorn in our sides.

Be aware that all executive get-togethers run longer than they should. If it's going well for the person running it, he'll want to keep it going. And if it's going badly for the person presiding, someone else will want to keep it going.

The best you can hope to do is to keep all meetings you control as short as possible. One way to abbreviate them is to get to the heart of the matter as expeditiously as you can. As the presiding officer, the first four things you should say at the meeting are "I heard that one," "I heard that one," "I heard that one," and "I heard that one, too."

Believe it or not, this technique will cut your meeting time by almost twenty minutes. How? Let me show you.

SETTING: *An office in which tables and chairs are obviously arranged for an upcoming meeting. You are seated in a position of power. The attendees file in and take their seats.*

ATTENDEE ONE. Hey, I heard a joke last night about a computer expert who took his secretary on a business trip and they had to room together . . .

YOU. I heard that one.

ATTENDEE ONE. Oh.

ATTENDEE TWO. Did you hear about the cross-eyed bull who saw a cow standing next to the water pump?

YOU. I heard that one.

ATTENDEE THREE. How about the two hippopotamuses who were standing outside of a dentist's office . . .

YOU. I heard that one.

ATTENDEE ONE. *(again)* At this same meeting, I heard
  another joke . . .

YOU. I heard that one, too.

End of Demonstration.

Now the meeting can begin, and you have saved an awful
lot of time up front.

Another helpful ploy is to try to schedule your meetings
before a catastrophe if at all possible. For instance, if a
strike is imminent, call your meeting half an hour before it
is to begin.

If one of the workers tells you that because the blueprint-
ing machine is in bad shape, a hose will break any minute,
spraying ammonia all over the office, and endangering the
well-being of the employees, quickly call a meeting.

If an electrical outlet is badly overloaded, the wires are
frayed, and an electrical fire is expected, notify your staff
that you want them to report to your office immediately.

I have even staged my own catastrophes. I will slip a few
bucks to a couple of my employees with instructions to
start punching one another in the face at a specified time
after my meeting begins. It causes a terrible hubbub
among the other workers, and the executives instantly pour
out of my office to see what is going on.

An infallible way to cut a meeting short, whether you're
running it or not, is to mention casually that you heard a
rumor that Mr. Bigwig, the ranking company official on the
corporate level, will be around to look in on the offices this
afternoon. Now, you don't know if this is a verified rumor or
not. In fact, you can even say that you heard it but know for a
fact that it is false—it won't make any difference. Those
executives will rush out of there in no time flat.

Just one last note. If you hate meetings as much as I do,
perhaps you too can rally against them. Try my aversion
therapy.

When I was a kid, my older brother caught me sneaking some cigarettes. Rather than telling our mom and dad or forbidding me to smoke, he gave his approval. He was delighted, he said, that I was learning to smoke.

He immediately went out and bought cartons of cigarettes for me to try—menthol and filtered, long and short, every kind imaginable. He also tossed in a few boxes of cigars and even some other smokable stuff, I think. Then he sat down and invited me to light up. He had me smoke one thing after another. He even invited friends of mine in to watch how well I smoked and how much I enjoyed it.

After several packs of cigarettes, I wanted to stop, but no, he insisted that I smoke everything. If I wanted to smoke, I should really smoke.

I turned many hues of green and probably a few colors that not even the rainbow had heard of, but still he wouldn't let up. There was so much to smoke and so little time in which to do it.

Well, after this experience I never touched another cigarette again. I did touch my brother, though. When I got older and bigger, I broke his jaw.

The lesson is clear: Have meetings for your staff every minute of the working day, and even a few at night. Hold meetings until they are coming out their ying-yangs.

I don't know if it will work or not, but we have to start somewhere. Those of us who hate these pagan rituals have to do *something* to stop them. Why don't we form an association and maybe have monthly meetings to see if we can stamp this out?

CHAPTER 6

Responsibility

or

An official assignment is like
a stop sign at an intersection—it loses
its authority once you pass it.

The hit or miss management theory concerning responsibility is so logical that those who oppose it, and there are a few, must resort to illogical arguments.

When I was a child, my mother always harped on me to wash behind my ears. Regardless of how dirty the rest of me was before my bath, the admonition was always the same: "Wash behind your ears." It was a mystery to me at the time because I never did anything with the area behind my ears that might get it inordinately unclean. My hands I could understand. I would make mud pies with my hands, or pick up things even though (again in my mother's words) I "didn't know where they had been." My torso would get filthy from sliding into second base on a baseball diamond entirely composed of cinders. My knees would get grubby from kneeling in the streets to play marbles and pitch pennies.

None of these areas were ever singled out by my parent, though, as requiring special attention. Behind the ears was the problem area all the time.

Did this place get dirtier than the rest of me? I never knew because it is impossible to see the back of your ears. I

tried, but it is impossible. Even with a mirror you can't see there, because somehow or another your head always gets in the way.

It was not until I was well past puberty and into maturity that the sagacity of my mother's directive dawned on me. It was a wisely form of misdirection. I used to employ a similar little gimmick on other kids my age: I'd hold up my right hand and say, "See this fist?"; then, as they focused their attention on it, I would punch them in the stomach with my left.

Mom was just as cagey. As soon as I was told to wash behind my ears, it became something I didn't want to do. However, I knew I had to do it because mom would inspect me after my bath. It was a cleverly chosen area, too, because of its inaccessibility. I couldn't see to make sure that it was clean enough to pass Mom's muster, and so I had to wash it . . . eventually.

Eventually is the key word here. Because I didn't want to do anything my mother told me was good for me but since I had to nonetheless, I would delay the inevitable. How would I do that? You guessed it—or if you didn't you're some kind of dummy—by spending more time scrubbing other parts of my body.

Do you see the shrewdness of this ploy? Had my mother demanded that I wash these other areas, I instinctively would have sloughed over them; but by picking some obscure, unimportant, unseen portion of my anatomy, she guaranteed a thorough scrubbing of those parts she really wanted immaculate. I would scour my hands and scrub my knees and rub away at my torso just to avoid doing justice to the area behind my ears.

But so deeply ingrained is the tradition that today, even though I know that "behind the ears" is a misdirective, I still scrub there thoroughly each morning. Even though the fallacy has been exposed in my mind, the maxim remains to taunt me. How does all of this apply? I'll tell you if you'll just be patient. I'm typing as fast as I can.

The opponents of *Hit or Miss Management* have as devious a scheme as my mother's that they work on us. "Every good manager must be able to handle responsibility"—this is drummed into every person who has ever filled out a job application or punched a time clock. You see, they catch us in our formative years, just as our parents did. They drum this into our brains before we have the capacity to analyze it. Later, even though it may be exposed as a sham, the admonition is embedded in our subconscious minds.

And responsibility is even harder to see than the area behind one's ears. If you really wanted to go to the trouble, you could hold a hand mirror behind your head while facing another mirror and get some kind of glimpse behind your ears. There is no mirror that will reflect responsibility, though.

What *is* responsibility anyway? Let me give you a hint. At Little Big Horn, it was General Custer's responsibility to defeat the Indians. On the *Titanic,* it was the captain's responsibility to be the last one off the ship. Are you beginning to discover a pattern here? Responsibility was what Bud Abbott always gave to Lou Costello when they were in any kind of jeopardy.

We managers would not do half the things that are required of us if upper management just said, "Do it." You can't talk a cow into walking into a slaughterhouse. You have to scare him from the outside. Cowboys have to scream and holler and wave their hats in the air. The hapless creature gets to thinking he'll be safer inside the slaughterhouse, so he gallops in—and gets clobbered right between the eyes with a mallet.

We are not dissimilar. Upper management diverts our attention with the word *responsibility,* and we rush headlong into the rubber mallet.

But why do we hear so many ambitious people say, "I want a job with more responsibility?" Because claiming to want more responsibility is actually a euphemism for want-

BOSS. Wilson [*that's you*], thanks for coming up to my office.

YOU. (*adroitly cheerful*) No problem at all, sir. What can I do for you?

BOSS. We're having a little problem with the vertical-lift mechanism. We can't get it to operate quickly enough to make it feasible.

YOU. (*acting surprised*) Really, sir?

BOSS. Now you know that this was my baby all along. I stuck my neck out with this one, but that's what I'm here for. I've always been the kind of executive who was never afraid to take chances.

YOU. (*cunningly sarcastic*) I know it was your baby, sir. I remember when you had me sign the report that you wrote.

BOSS. (*feigning graciousness*) I'm not one to hog the glory either. But in any case, the board wants to abandon this plan.

YOU. That's a shame, sir.

BOSS. (*nervously angry*) It's catastrophic, Wilson. It could mean a black mark on our [*notice the inclusion of you in the negative sentence*] department.

YOU. (*scared*) Yes, sir.

BOSS. *No,* sir. I refuse to let that happen. I convinced them that with a little more time we can solve this dilemma. And YOU are the perfect man for it.

YOU. (*in slightly cracking voice*) Me, sir?

BOSS. (*beginning to feel his old self again—patting you on back*) I have confidence in you, Wilson. If anyone can do it, you can. You will be in complete charge of this

ing less. In reality what these people are saying is, "I wa
job where I can GIVE OUT more responsibility." T
want more *authority* so that they can avoid more *respo
bility.*

You see, responsibility in management is like a chain
ter. Once you receive it, you quickly forward it to fiv
ten other people. You never keep it. Like the chain le
it ominously promises grave misfortunes unless you qu
transfer it to your underlings.

Herein lies the secret of how you, as a manager, sh
handle responsibility. You should fight euphemism
euphemism. Your superior is adept at handling respon
ity, so you must become skilled at *delegating authority.*

The chain of power here should be fairly obvious.
boss sees a bullet speeding toward him. He has his
tary buzz you, and he promptly gives you some respo
ity. In whatever words he chooses to disguise his m
he is saying, in effect, "I have a bullet speeding towa
and I need your help immediately." Your reply is, "Y
I'll send some of my people up right away." You ha
delegated authority.

Keep the above paragraph in mind always. Reduc
what your superior says to you to that basic para
Have it done in script, Perma-Plaqued, and dis
prominently on your desk. All authority in busi
summed up by that paragraph.

Don't let verbiage confuse you. Consider the fo
one-act play.

*SETTING: The boss's office, three floors up from yo
naturally. The boss is pacing nervously, like a man
expecting a newborn or a husband who thinks his
is expecting a newborn. His tie is irreverently loo
which is uncharacteristic for a man of his stature
enter, he struggles to regain some of his composu
speaks.*

project. It will be your RESPONSIBILITY to see this thing through and make it work.

YOU. But, sir . . .

BOSS. We don't have time for "buts," Wilson. This is a wonderful opportunity. Now here's what I want you to do.

(At this point, the dialogue becomes too technical for anyone not in the vertical-lift business, so instead of using the technical terms, I will write out what the boss is actually saying to Wilson.)

BOSS. I want you to take as many workers as you need, within a reasonable budget, then I want you to design a giant sling. Then I want you, Wilson, to put your ass in it. . . .

Well, you get the picture. All of the dialogue is camouflage for the basic "I have a bullet speeding toward me, and I want you to jump in front of it" gambit.

Notice, also, that sometimes the responsibility is disguised as a challenge. The boss praises your skills and claims he can't function without them. What he is really saying is that he is up against a brick wall and he wants you to break it down for him. "You can do it," he eulogizes, "just use your head." He almost literally wants you to ram down a brick wall with your noggin. Should you do just that, the boss would go to his superior and say, "Well, I've had a big breakthrough." He'd get the pat on the back, but nobody would notice that there was nothing showing above your collar anymore.

However, *Hit or Miss Management* will never permit any of its disciples to be cornered by an establishment manager. You have a way out. You can delegate authority. Consider act two of our one-act play.

SETTING: *Your own office, three floors down from the boss's. Pacing, you nervously wait to receive Walker, your underling, whom you've just had your secretary summon. As he enters, you speak.*

YOU. Walker [*that's him*], thanks for coming up to my office.

WALKER. *(adroitly cheerful)* No problem at all, sir. What can I do for you?

YOU. Walker, we're having a little problem with the vertical-lift mechanism. . . .

Well, you probably know how act two of our one-act play ends. You simply pass the responsibility on to Walker. It may seem a bit cruel, but if Walker has read *Hit or Miss Management,* he in turn will know how to handle it. If Walker has not read *Hit or Miss Management,* he deserves everything he gets.

CHAPTER 7

Report writing

or
Any document that's worth
writing is worth writing twice by employing
the art of double talk.

Sometime after the armadillo is born, he discovers that he is hungry. Somewhere in that tiny consciousness he knows that the food is out there in the cruel world and has to be foraged for. (Armadillos don't mind ending sentences with a preposition.) Armadillos don't have other armadillos bringing them food from door to door. His intuition also tells him that the world is not always a safe place. He knows that, should he venture forth, there are other animals out there searching for their next meal, and he may be it.

Now the armadillo looks at his body and says to himself, "This doesn't look like it's too streamlined. With this cute, round little body and attractive but unquestionably short legs, I ain't gonna outrun too many creatures." With a little further inspection, he realizes that he also isn't too highly ranked in the ferocity department and is not going to scare many predators off.

So he says to himself, again (armadillos like to talk to themselves), "I think I'll grow a thick skin of heavy armor plate. No way am I going to go out looking for food in my skivvies."

The moral of our little nature study is that the wise manager would never journey forth from the sanctuary of his office in his executive skivvies. When he does venture forth from his thickly carpeted nest and makes a decision, like the little armadillo, he recognizes that he is exposing his frail little self to various dangers, so he wraps himself in a protective covering.

What is this raiment, this cloak, this suit of armor? What can protect an otherwise vulnerable manager from—to coin a phrase—the slings and arrows of outrageous fortune? If you had read the chapter heading you'd know.

The report is the manager's protective shell. His underlings do their research, reach their conclusions, document their findings, and affix their signatures to said document. Now the manager is safe in his armor. He protects his managerial skivvies with a thick layer of employees.

Report Writing: The Educational Value of

Should your finished report serve the purpose of enlightening others? Absolutely not. Oh, I know that's what your boss asked for, but that is not what he wanted. If protective shields were meant to educate, the armadillo would be wearing an encyclopedia instead of a thick external shell.

Your finished composition should be a masterpiece of circumlocution. It should ramble and tangentize incessantly. A paraphrasing of Winston Churchill's famous quote should define your finished product: "Never before has so much been written for so many and said so little."

Report Writing: The Use of Statistics Therein

Every report must contain numbers. Remember that's all top executives really read. Words bore them, but numbers titillate them. If meetings are orgasmic to them, complicated numbers are masturbatory.

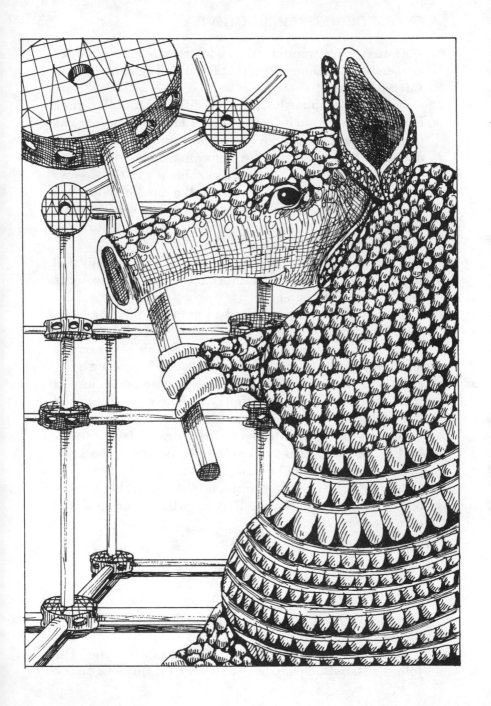

Statistics are wonderfully and conveniently versatile. Remember the same bottle that is half full can also be considered half empty.

Being the fabulously malleable instruments that they are, statistics should be made to work for you. They are like an adult set of Tinker Toys. Numbers and decimal points and addition and subtraction signs are thrown into a heap. One person can pick up these mathematical Tinker Toys and make a giraffe. Another can use the same playthings to create a hippopotamus. A third person might construct a truck, a bridge, a teddy bear. The components are the same for everyone. It's the assembly that varies.

To embed in your mind the value of the flexibility of numbers and statistics, memorize the following parable and learn well its moral.

There was once a man who had to fly for the first time, but he was deathly afraid of air travel. He called the airlines and asked what the chances were of a bomb being on the same plane that he'd be on. They replied, "Oh, maybe five million to one." He wasn't crazy about those odds. Sure, it was a long shot, he figured, but what if he were that one in five million?

He called the airline back and posed this question: "What are the chances of two bombs being on the same plane?" The clerk kind of laughed, but politely answered, "Oh, maybe five hundred million to one." He liked these odds a little better. Now he'll fly anywhere, but he always carries one bomb with him.

A Sample Report

Now that you know the basic philosophy behind the *Hit or Miss Management* report, allow me to illustrate with a sample document I've composed myself.

Permit me to set the hypothetical scene for you. The John B. Stalk Company has fallen on hard financial times, and its board of directors has opted to bail the company out by selling the company cow to the local slaughterhouse.

However, on the way to the consummation of the sale, an interesting alternative was proposed. A vendor offered to buy the cow. The purchase price was a bag of magic beans.

This offer is now being considered. A report on the feasibility of the arrangement is in the works.

The *Hit or Miss Management* annotated version of this report, composed by your author, is included here for your edification and future reference.

On the Relative Merits of Selling the Company Cow for One Bag of Beans (Magic) As Compared to a Decision Previously Made by the August Board of Directors, Considering Both the Long-Term and the Short-Term Benefits in Light of the Company's Present Financial Requirements

by Eugene R. Perret

Purpose:
The purpose of this report is to compare the relative merits of selling the company cow for one bag of beans (magic) to the decision previously made by the august board of directors to sell the company cow for a fair price to the local slaughterhouse in order to gain sufficient cash flow to assist the company through its present financial impasse.

The nature of this report is to provide the research necessary for the board to reevaluate its previous decision in light of the new counter proposal. No effort will be made to usurp the decision making of the august board.

[You might as well enhance your position by buttering them up. If they were any good at making decisions, the company wouldn't be going broke now.]

Methods of Comparison:
No option in this report will be considered feasible unless

it measures up to the profit margin of the department managed by the author of this report, Eugene R. Perret.

[These numbers, of course, could have been twisted to mean anything. Use them to help your cause.]

This is, admittedly, a rigid requirement since the profit-over-cost record of said department averaged 0.03 above the company-wide median. The differential from this department's profit margin to the lowest of the entire company was 6.2 percent, which is probably the largest in the history of the company, with the obvious exception of the time the entire machine shop was burned down by angry welders.

[None of this has anything to do with the report, but you've got to blow your own horn.]

Options:
(A) Sell the cow to the slaughterhouse.
(B) Sell the cow for the beans.
(C) Obviously, we could also keep the cow, but this would return us to the condition that existed before the august board of directors decided that the cow must be sold. We would simply be nullifying a decision carefully and sagely made.

[Butter them up—they hand out promotions.]

There may, of course, be other options that the board of directors may consider at a later time. For instance, we might sell the cow for the beans on a lease-back arrangement. However, our interest in the cow is for sale to a slaughterhouse. It would be difficult to lease a beast that has been cut up into bite-size pieces.

[Always allow them a way out. Don't make any definite pronouncements in your report.]

Option A (selling the cow to the slaughterhouse):
The merits of this option are totally unchanged. They have all been covered under a separate report, "On the Benefits to Be Gained by Selling the Company Cow to the Local

Slaughterhouse and the Effect of the Financial Gain Thus Realized on the Survival of the Company."

That report, written by the manager of another department, perhaps compared the merits to his own departmental profit average, which is somewhat lower than the record achieved by the author of this report.

[Toot your own horn, baby, and get that other guy.]

Nevertheless, we are sure that the august board of directors considered that factor in making their previous learned decision.

Therefore, the remainder of this report will concentrate on the benefits to be realized under Option B, to give the august board of directors sufficient background to reevaluate.

[Let them make the decision.]

The Price (one bag of beans [magic]):
There is no standardization of the number of beans contained in a bag, as there is with the common terms dozen (12) or gross (a dozen dozens, or 144).

In order to approximate the actual purchase price in this case, we experimented with a bag similar in size to the one offered in exchange for the company cow. We placed different types of beans in this bag and came up with the results shown in Table 1.

We also have no idea as to the actual size of a magic bean. (Our research into this will be covered later in the report.)

Conclusions:
Since it is doubtful that a seller would pack a bag tightly, we would estimate that the number of the beans (magic) in the purchase bag is somewhere between 3.3333 and 5.45 beans.

Value (actual):
The value of the cow was very roughly approximated in the previous report, "On the Benefits to Be Gained by Selling the Company Cow to the Local Slaughterhouse and the

TABLE 1

APPROXIMATION
OF THE NUMBER OF BEANS IN ONE BAG.

TYPE OF BEAN	LIGHTLY PACKED	MODERATELY PACKED	TIGHTLY PACKED
Lima	2	4	8
Baked	5	8	17
Mexican Jumping	4	6	12
Garbanzo	4	6	13
Butter	2	4	9
Navy	3	4.7	10
Average	3.3333	5.45	11.5

Effect of the Financial Gain Thus Realized on the Survival
of the Company."

[You got that guy again.]

This report will concentrate on studying the value of the
beans to be used in the purchase.

There exists very little empirical data on the value of
magic beans. We scoured magic catalog after magic catalog.
The results of our study are as follows:

Patriotic Color-changing Beans: You show your friends
five bright red beans, place them in the cup provided with
the trick, and shake them—they come out blue. Amaze
them once more: when you shake the cup again, the beans
are pure white. Do it a third time, and you wind up with
red, white, and blue beans.
All beans included. $7.95

The Obedient Bean: Show your friends a common,
ordinary bean. Let them inspect it, then have them place
it on a table. You tell it to roll over and watch the
amazement in your friends' eyes when the bean obeys
each of your commands.
No wires or strings. $5.25

Magic Mating Beans: This trick comes with a script for a
cute love story, or a more adult version if company is not
mixed. No matter where you place the beans, they will
immediately be attracted to each other.
Fun 'n' laughs for all. $3.00

Wet and Dry Beans: Open a bean-like container, fill it with
salt, say the magic words, and the salt turns to water.
Two magic beans, some sleight of hand. $5.25

Multiplying Beans: Place a bean under a cup. Each time
the cup is lifted, the beans magically multiply.
No sleight of hand. $7.75

Conclusions:
In the interest of economy, these magic beans were not
purchased. However, the number of beans in each trick

was approximated and an average price for a magic bean arrived at as follows:

$$\frac{\text{total purchase price}}{\text{total number of beans (estimate)}} = \text{price per magic bean}$$

$$\frac{\$29.20}{32} = \$0.91$$

Therefore, according to our calculations, each actual magic bean costs $0.91. However, our research shows that 80% of the price of a magic trick is for the instructions contained therein. If we again use the above calculation, then, each bean actually costs only $0.182.

Since we approximated that there were between 3.3333 and 5.45 beans in the purchase bag, we are talking of an actual value of $0.60–$0.9919.

[All this is nonsense, of course, but they'll love it because executives find numbers and figures titillating.]

Value (supposed): [Don't make any decisions for them.] It is doubtful that the august board of directors would consider selling the cow for a maximum of $0.9919. Therefore, we should consider the "supposed" value of the magic beans, to wit (and we quote the vendor), "They will grow and reach a giant's kingdom where there is a goose that lays golden eggs."

Assuming the veracity of the vendor's statement, although the author warns the directors that the purchase comes "as is" with no guarantees or warranties of any substance, we still have to investigate (a) the growth rate of beanstalks and (b) the value of golden eggs.

Growth Rate of Beanstalks:
Inquiries concerning the workings of magic beans were made at several magic shops. However, it was discovered that the secrets of all magic apparatus are carefully

guarded and given out only to fellow magicians. In light of the company's present financial problems, it was deemed unwise to join the International Brotherhood of Magicians simply for its research value. Therefore, we studied the growth rates of other beans. The results are shown in Figure 1.

Even under the most generous of growth approximations, if we assume that the most ideal conditions of climate, rainfall, etc., exist, it would take a minimum of thirty years for a beanstalk to grow high enough to reach the castle of the lowliest of giants.

It is for the august board of directors to determine if the long-term benefits are worth this rather extensive wait.

[Again, let them decide.]

Value of Golden Eggs:
Unfortunately, there is little concrete information available on golden eggs. This writer again had to approximate their value. However, over the past few

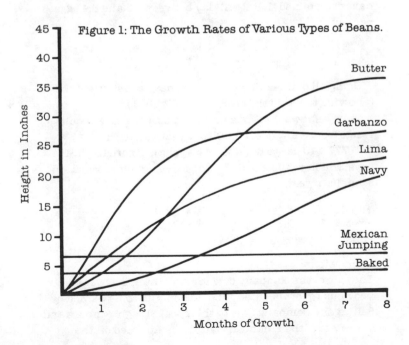

Figure 1: The Growth Rates of Various Types of Beans.

years, the estimates he has made in the normal course of business forecasting have proved to be accurate to within 0.3 percent, which is well within even the most scientific allowances of acceptability.

These questions were considered: (a) Is the egg solid? (b) How many eggs does the goose lay daily? (c) What is the value of the gold? The calculations follow.

[Great pat on the back. If you don't do it, who will?]

If the egg is solid, the approximated weight is 12 ounces. If the egg is merely a golden shell, the estimated weight is 0.9 ounces.

The price of gold must be estimated for the period thirty years hence, when it is predicted that the stalk will reach the giant's castle. Considering inflation, the relative scarcity of gold, and several other factors, we have determined that it will be no lower than $900 per ounce and no higher than $1,800 per ounce.

Again, since we know little about the goose itself, we have determined that it will lay between 1.3 and 3.4 eggs per day.

[It's actually between 1 and 4, but remember that these decimals titillate.]

Using all of this information, we have constructed the following table of relative returns (Table 2).

Table 2 shows that, on a yearly basis, the return could range from a low of $123,201 per year to a high of $25,777,440 per year. (Note: The year is figured as 351 days, which would allow the goose two weeks of vacation each fiscal year.)

[You might as well figure this in, because otherwise the financially beleaguered company may try to save by eliminating vacations—including yours.]

Conclusions:
The sale of the company cow for slaughter as covered in a previous report entitled "On the Benefits to Be Gained by Selling the Company Cow to the Local Slaughterhouse and the Effect of the Financial Gain Thus Realized on the

TABLE 2

Type of Egg	Value per Egg		Return per Day	
Gold Egg Shell Only (0.9 oz./egg)	At $900/oz.	$ 810	1.3 EPD*	$ 1,053
			3.4 EPD	2,754
	At $1,800/oz.	1,620	1.3 EPD	2,106
			3.4 EPD	5,508
Solid Gold (12 oz./egg)	At $900/oz.	10,800	1.3 EPD	14,040
			3.4 EPD	36,720
	At $1,800/oz.	21,600	1.3 EPD	28,080
			3.4 EPD	73,440

*Eggs per Day

Survival of the Company" would provide immediate profits for the company. Even though those profits were only sketchily drawn out in the previous report, they would accrue more quickly than any others.

The sale of the cow for the bag of magic beans would produce much more substantial results, as the acquisition of said beans would give us a potential gain of over $25 million per year, but there would be considerable delay before these returns would be realized (a minimum wait of thirty years).

This report would not consider encroaching upon the august board of directors' decision-making policy. We merely point out the long-term and short-term benefits of each option.

[There is no conclusion here at all—excellent.]

Addendum:

Despite the economic factors herein contained, there are several questions of property rights inherent in this sale. For example, does buying a bag of magic beans give us the right to trespass on a giant's property, and does it give us proprietary rights over the eggs laid by the golden goose? These questions have been turned over to the legal department, and their report, as yet untitled, will be forthcoming.

[Great! Get off of the hook even more.]

Respectfully submitted,

[Don't even make the signature readable.]

CHAPTER 8

Budgets

or
Money is the root of all evil
and every year upper management makes you
pull it out by the roots.

Budgets are a fact of life. *Hit or Miss Management* is still a dream. Until it becomes a reality, we must cope with the so-called facts of life. If we want to journey to Utopia (i.e., Hit or Miss Management Land), we must pay the carfare.

In the ideal *Hit or Miss Management* scheme, budgets are nonexistent. Remember, our theories are drawn from nature itself, and nowhere does money exist in nature. Why can the gazelle run fast and leap far? Because he doesn't have to carry loose change around in his pocket. The leopard can wait for his prey any place he chooses without worrying about putting a coin in the parking meter. Sure, squirrels store their nuts for the winter, but they don't have to stand in line and fill out a slip with a ball-point pen that doesn't write in order to make a withdrawal.

But your author, in his wisdom, not only maps out a business Camelot for you but teaches you how to deal with the complicated and unnecessary economic practices that exist today. I will tell you about budgets. Why do you think I called this chapter "Budgets"? Geez.

As a lad, I remember a candy store on our corner, its exterior as humble as the rest of the neighborhood. The windows were painted to relieve the owner of the burden of setting up displays in them, and, of course, they had the ubiquitous BB hole emanating cracks fortified with electrical tape. The steps were covered with stains of various sizes and colors, relics of delicacies consumed, with not much gentility, right there on the premises. The stone facade was covered with neighborhood apothegms, the graffiti of a past age. It was generally more refined than today's version because it rarely contained obscenities and was written in chalk, so that the rains would clear the slate for the writings of another.

However, as is the case with people, the real beauty of a candy store is on the inside. This place had a cooler full of refreshingly ice-cold sodas. It boasted a freezer housing eight to twelve different flavors of ice cream and offered both plain and sugar cones. It had a glass case full of the most scrumptious candies ever made, some of my old favorites and many exciting new varieties. For those who enjoyed reading while they ate, row upon row of comic books were displayed. In fact, this place had only one negative drawback—everything in it cost money.

Being a youngster in South Philly didn't pay very good money in those days. Of course, the expenses weren't that high either. A nickel "pimple ball," as we used to call it, would provide entertainment for an entire block of children for several weeks. After a tough game of block ball, though, the entire gang would emigrate to the corner store and cool off with a bottle of soda. If you didn't have the capital to finance your very own bottle, you had to rely on "swiggies." A swiggie meant that if someone was benevolent enough, he might let you have a mouthful of his elixir. There was no way this would satisfy a youngster's thirst, though, so funding had to be found.

That's when I would go to my mom with the recurrent plea, "Mom, can I have a nickel?" Mom would never say no, but she had some answers that were just as effective: "Do you think money grows on trees?"; "Do you think I'm made of money?"; and my all-time favorite, "If I had a nickel, I'd sit up all night and watch it."

Getting money in a company is not unlike getting five cents from my Mom. When the technical jargon is translated, it reduces to a corporate "If we had that kind of money, we'd sit up all night and watch it."

However, in your managerial capacity, you're in the same boat I was in as a child. You have no corporate income of your own. You can't manufacture money, and if you could you probably wouldn't give it to your company. And in the business world economic swiggies are nonexistent. All the corporate funding necessary to carry out your duties and perform the functions required of you come from the company's generosity. If you want funds you must ask for them. You must tug the skirts of your corporate mother and plead, "Mommy, mommy, can I have a nickel?"

In business, of course, financial requests must be much more formalized and ceremonial than this. At least once each fiscal year you will have to account to someone for all the nickels they have generously bestowed on your department and request funds for the coming year. This custom of groveling and niggardliness is called the "budget review."

Since as a manager you can't avoid becoming involved in the humiliation of budgets, there are a few things you ought to know. First of all, before you beg for new money, it's a good idea to realize that as far as the company is concerned, you did not *spend* last year's budget—you wasted it. With the guilt of this condemnation weighing heavily on your head, you must solicit funds for next year's operation.

After you've been through enough of these degrading ordeals, it becomes obvious that what management wants from you and what they are asked to deliver to their bosses is twice the output at half the cost.

The irony of this entire pageant is that the corporation's

outward display of frugality is actually a mask for some ludicrous prodigality. These budgetary inquisitions actually cost the company more money than they like to admit. Follow the subtlety of my thinking.

Each department must survive this economic gauntlet in order to function for the coming fiscal year. Each manager is expected to solicit funds with the devotion and determination of a Jerry Lewis hosting his annual telethon. Probably more effort is devoted each year to the enhancement of departmental budgets than to any other project.

The superiors who sit in on this court-martial-like meeting expect to be given a spectacular presentation. Your importuning for budgetary blessings must be accompanied by dazzling and effective charts. Like in a court of law, where the dexterity of the lawyers is weighed more heavily than the guilt or innocence of the defendant, so, too, the ingenuity displayed in your chart work is more important than your actual need for funds.

Consequently, the wise executive has his staff working feverishly on research, statistical manipulation, and chart art. All of this requires many man-hours, woman-hours, and computer-hours, and each man, woman, and computer must be remunerated. The salary and/or electricity for all this effort is paid by the same company that is sitting in judgment of your economic expertise.

I think back again to my childhood days (the nights are none of your business) and consider what might have happened had I had the foresight, the ambition, and the wherewithal to step forward with a clever documentation and colorful charts when asking my mom for a nickel. Had I gotten her to sit still long enough to listen to my skillful discourse on why I needed the coin, the result probably would have been, "If I had a nickel, I'd sit up all night and watch it."

Upper management may respond similarly and reject your flashy presentation. Why? Because they know that, traditionally, you will request more than you need. They always did. They still do. Why should they assume that you're any better? Your request is denied. Do you think this company is made of money?

You may be instructed to go back and prepare another report, one that is more in line with "reality." They give you an A for creativity but a zero for budget. Now, this is clever. They think you're spending too much, so they command you to go back and spend more in order to show them that you can spend less.

And so you do. You spend twice what you should in order to merit half of what you need.

Here is my suggestion—the hit or miss manager's approach to getting everything you want from budget reviews.

Go to your next budget meeting naked. Not literally, of course, but not festooned with all the ceremonial paraphernalia of documentation and statistical reports and multicolored charts. Just mentally calculate roughly what you will need to run your department effectively. Round it off. Up or down. It doesn't matter. When you stand before your judges, simply announce what the figure is.

After they've recovered from the shock of your brazenness, they will ask you to justify your request.

Now you've got them. Tell them quite candidly that you can't. It may take even longer for them to recuperate from this bombshell, but wait and then offer to make a deal. You told them what you want, and you both know that they will cut it in half. Okay. Working from that basis, impress on them that you have saved them quite a bit of moola by not trying to validate your budget demands. Specify the man-, woman-, and computer-hours saved and the money you have refused to squander on research and chart making. (You might even have a chart showing the comparative amounts.) Then offer to split the difference. You'll accept half of what you asked, plus half of what you saved. That way, they save money, and you are rewarded with more than you would otherwise have gotten. Everybody wins. I'm okay. You're okay. They're okay. Okay?

If they say no, take my word for it, you simply weren't sufficiently brazen. This method works. I'm sure of it, and I beg you to try it. Be sure to write or call me with your results, though, because I've never had the courage to try it myself.

CHAPTER 9

Use of time

or
If you want something done, give it to
a busy man. He'll be too bogged down with
work to think up an excuse not to do it.

Time is a beautiful and wondrous entity. It's immutable, unalterable. It cannot be compressed and absolutely refuses to be elongated. It is impossible to bend into different shapes. No one can machine it into different designs. It is the least malleable creation of anything known to humankind. Have I made my point?

Time has the ultimate in bargaining strength. Time doesn't need us; we need time. Therein lies the secret to time's potency. Each individual, each department, each corporation has to count time as one of its most valuable assets. Everything anyone tries to do must be measured in terms of time. (Cost is also a substantial consideration for businesses, but it would be moot unless accompanied by time. If you don't have the time to do something, why concern yourself with how much it would have cost? These are tough questions, I know.)

It amuses me when I read haughty management books that tell us how we can outsmart time, how we can get more of it or alter it to suit our needs. BALDERDASH.

All of these ingenious schemes we come up with to alter, change, stretch, or bend time are fruitless, yet learned men and women continue to promulgate them. Do things in a certain order, plan your goals, block out interruptions, keep records, and so on, both ad infinitum and ad nauseam.

I recently scanned (who has time to read?) a book by R. Alec Mackenzie called *The Time Trap: How to Get More Done in Less Time*. It contains nine chapters and one appendix covering some very clever ways of organizing your time. To apply all of his directives properly, you'd had to have begun at about the time Christ was born.

Hit or Miss Management again recommends nature's way of using time: simply use it. Look at every frame of film that Jacques Cousteau has shot beneath the sea. You will never see a shark making a list of things to do today. Visit any zoo in the country. In none of them will you see a sheet of paper hanging up in the gorilla's cage that reads:

1. Play with tire.
2. Throw waste matter at the visitors.
3. Pick insects out of mate's fur.
4. Pound on chest in a show of strength.
5. Eat several bananas.

List making is as unnatural as it is ludicrous, so why bother with it? Yet it is ubiquitous in all of these silly books on saving time, and it appears everywhere in them, too. Instead of making lists, you should just do whatever you have to do. Then you can use the time you would have used to make lists playing tennis or something.

Incidentally, the volume you are reading was delivered to the publisher on time. The manuscript of R. Alec Mackenzie, on the other hand, is rumored to have required several extensions before it reached the press. Every time the publishers called for more pages, they got another list.

Remember the words of a famous teacher: "Those who can, do. Those who can't, make lists."

CHAPTER 10

Scheduling

or
The difference between "scheduled
date of completion" and "date of completion"
is the same as the difference between
"chicken" and "chicken-pox."

In any business establishment you visit, a cursory inspection of the walls will reveal some kind of scheduling chart. They're as common as a shovel in a stable. Office walls fairly flaunt the complicated and intricate scheduling diagram. It displays itself with pride, silently pronouncing to the world, "Look how organized we are. We have a schedule."

Executives promote the myth that scheduling is difficult and involved. Do other management writers contradict this? No. Typically, they ignore the topic totally. (Typically . . . totally—that's nice writing.) My extensive library of management-practice volumes contains not a single reference to scheduling.

For once, these experts are right. Why? Because they know that the scheduling phenomenon exists but serves no real managerial purpose, and therefore they wisely omit it from their writings.

The unicorn certainly exists, but you won't find a drawing of its internal organs in any biology book. And yes, Virginia, there is a Santa Claus, but you won't find him listed in *Who's Who,* nor, Virginia, will you find a tax return of his filed with the Internal Revenue Service, which is an even more conclusive proof of existence than a valid birth certificate.

Hit or Miss Management, however, has more audacity than the establishment hacks. (You guys know who you are, and by now so do my readers.) We don't just ignore the topic. We don't allow misconceptions about scheduling to continue just because we are afraid to deal with them. I expose it for what it is. To be an effective business writer, one must confront these managerial fables. A good cattle rancher can't be afraid of bullshit.

In fact, scheduling is the easiest duty that a manager has. It consists of taking an assignment and writing after it a month, a date, and a year. Naturally, though, that's not all there is to it. Whoever gave you the assignment will not be satisfied with the date you promise. So you haggle and you negotiate and then you write down another month, date, and year. *That's* all there is to it.

A classic story will illustrate my point. There once was a woman who was cleaning out her parents' attic. This hadn't been done in decades, and she enjoyed discovering the many antique relics that were hidden away. In cleaning out an old chest, this woman discovered a tattered, brittle ticket from a shoe-repair shop. The due date, which could barely be read, was sixty-eight years ago.

Oddly enough, the repair shop still existed, so the woman took the ticket stub to the shop and presented it to the proprietor. She recounted the story and inquired if the shoes might still be there. The repairman carefully inspected the fragile bit of cardboard and then went into the back of the store. He returned nodding his head yes. The woman, stunned, said, "You still have those shoes here?" The shoe repairman said, "That's right. They'll be ready next Tuesday."

That, my friend, is a brief lesson in managerial scheduling. Promise any date you want, but don't actually do the work until someone starts pestering you for it.

Some of you may complain that this *Hit or Miss Management* suggestion seems lackadaisical. I don't know why this book attracts all the complainers. At times I half wish some of my readers would go out and see a movie instead. Mine is not a careless method, or, I should say, it is certainly no more careless than any other system that you might be using.

Since the beginning of time, no schedule has ever been accurate. No project has ever been completed on the day it was guaranteed. No piece of furniture has ever arrived on the delivery date. No child has ever been born nine months to the day from the moment of conception. Even nature's own twenty-four-hour viruses sometimes stay twenty to thirty minutes past their check-out time. All right, so a few swallows do return to Capistrano on the assigned date each year, but they're fanatic swallows who do it mostly for the publicity. (Some birds will do anything to get their picture in the paper.)

There simply is no solid documentation of any schedule ever having been adhered to. Now anything that doesn't work all of the time has got to be wrong—so why waste time with it?

Keep in mind that God created the world in six days, but he promised it in four.

dining-room buffet. Writing paper and envelopes could be found in the top drawer of this buffet. Schoolbooks were always scrunched into the server. Things that belonged to an individual member of the family but could roughly be described as miscellaneous were always found in that individual's "sock drawer." My fielder's glove and baseballs were at home only on the right-hand side of the buffet.

If you wanted to borrow my fielder's glove (and you'd better keep your hands off it—or else), you went to the right-hand side of the buffet. If it wasn't there it was lost. You need look no further. There was no other spot in the house where it could conceivably be.

These traditional places were so inviolate that if you accidentally put my fielder's glove on the left-hand side of the buffet, the buffet would immediately regurgitate the offending object.

And so it is with everything in the universe, be it household item or vital business document. There is a place where it belongs. Put it there and look for it there, and all your filing problems will go away.

So long as things are put where they naturally belong, recovering them is no problem. File them alphabetically or numerically, and you are just looking for trouble. The natural order seems to take offense when we try to usurp its powers. Periodically, mom would have something that was extra special. She would say, "I'll put this someplace where we'll be sure to find it." That object would never be seen again. Place something where it doesn't naturally belong, and nature annihilates it.

Hit or Miss Management suggests using the same filing and recovery system as my mom. Then when you want something, simply ask yourself, "Where did I put it last?" After all, if you're not interested enough in a project to remember where you put it last, you shouldn't be working on that project in the first place.

CHAPTER 12

Employees

or
Thank God for the little people.
Without them we'd have to do
the work ourselves.

The index of Drucker's book lists six pages for cost-reduction programs, and four separate listings for profits cover ten more pages. In the same book there is no listing at all for employees. He has the temerity to title his opus *Managing for Results*. What the hell is he managing?

I agree you can lead a horse to water, but not if you don't have a horse.

Hit or Miss Management believes that a manager's first duty is to get that next R/P. By now all my faithful readers know that. But *Hit or Miss Management* also recognizes that some work has to get done. We certainly don't recommend that the manager do it. His underlings must.

It's a *Hit or Miss Management* axiom: To get to the top of the heap, first you must have a heap.

Not too long ago I became interested in vitamins and food supplements. In my research I discovered something called *acidophilus*, a strain of bacteria that lives in the intestinal tract and while there works to promote and maintain a normal intestinal flora.

It's a therapeutic little animal that works hard for our benefit. However, upon learning of it, many thoughts struck me. Why would any living creature accept work like this? The hours are intolerable, the wages minimal, and the working conditions horrendous.

I am repulsed by the whole idea—not so much by the fact that the intestine performs a certain biological function, but rather by the knowledge that there are little living beings in that part of my body who are actually doing gardening there.

I wish I had not learned of their presence. For the sake of my health, I want them to stay and continue their distasteful labors, but I would rather not be aware of them. I would rather my intestines dispatch their tasks without my knowing who or what is doing which.

Why do I mention this biological phenomenon in the middle of this tome? Because this is the way most executives feel about their employees.

CHAPTER 13

Can you be a manager and a buddy?

or
Remember that you are intrinsically superior to employees. If managers and workers were the same thing, there wouldn't be two different words for it.

Hit or Miss Management refuses to look down its nose at the employees and to ignore the underlings as have all of my revered predecessors in the field of executive literature. In keeping with its realistic approach to management, we recognize the true worth of the worker . . . as a tool to getting your next R/P.

The manager has many tools available to him. When he sits at his desk he has a calendar, a notebook, pens and pencils, a stapler, a desk calculator, perhaps even a computer of some sort. He also has employees. Employees are tools of the trade. They are to the manager what a nail is to a carpenter, what a wrench is to a plumber, what fertilizer is to a farmer.

The employee, however, is somewhat misleading. A nail looks like a nail. A wrench resembles a wrench. Certainly fertilizer is not easily mistaken for something else. But the employee has the ability to look like a person. Don't be fooled, though. These aren't people; these are tools of your trade. The implements of your profession are best used dispassionately.

Some workers are even more adept than others at impersonating people. They are witty, charming, have winning personalities, and display a great deal of personal magnetism. One could almost like them if one didn't know better.

For the manager, though, liking them must be avoided at all costs.

Should you find yourself slipping into a personal relationship with one of your underlings, you must immediately find a means of counteracting it.

Don't misunderstand. This is not a condemnation of the worker. It is not meant to impugn his character, his personality, or his capacity for friendship with others. It is merely a caution that managers have no business getting involved with their employees.

Can you imagine the results if plumbers or carpenters became involved with any of their tools? Picture a carpenter who has a favorite nail. If he wants to use only that nail all the time, he would never construct anything that would stay together. Suppose there is a plumber who has a falling out with his wrench. He grows to hate that wrench and refuses to use it. He'd spend the entire day trying to disconnect pipes with his teeth. Of course, a farmer who becomes attached to her fertilizer is just too absurd to consider.

Some workers have a variety of clever disruptive devices that add to their illusion of being real people. They have a home life. They may even have a wife or husband who needs taking care of, children with bad teeth, pets with large appetites, and large mortgages on their houses. This is all very quaint—almost human—but as the well-known folk song says, "That's their misfortune and none of your own."

The much-maligned captains of ancient slave ships had the right idea. They brought their workers in and gave them a place of business, a seat with an oar. There were no frills to distract the rowers from their task. They provided enough food to sustain them and ample time to sleep. Even the uniforms were kept simple—a loincloth around the waist. Other than that they were there simply to row. Just to provide the ship with motion and not to worry about anything else.

Could you visualize what a difficult task it would be for the man with the whip if he had to stop every few seats to talk to the slaves about their problems at home? "How's the family? Oh, I'm sorry to hear that your wife is in the hospital. And your boy is flunking geometry? Aw, that's terrible. And the cat ran away? That must be difficult." The boat would never get anywhere. Clearly an impossible situation.

Even those workers who accept the reality of the situation will still try to deceive you by appealing to your sense of humanity. They might concede that they are merely implements to you and not really human entities, but they persist in the belief that you ought to care about their families. One might casually mention that the dog has been sick and expect you to reduce his quota for the week. Another will tell you that his children are having a tough time in school and anticipate some leniency regarding his work output for the day.

BALDERDASH. Invite them to reread their job applications. Challenge them to show you where it asks them how their children are doing in school. Dare them to find on there any reference to their spouse's health. Have them check over their job description and search out any paragraph that hints that their duties will be lessened if their dog comes down with the flu.

Don't be sucked into their maudlin sham. Call on whatever mental visualization you selected to remind yourself that all of your workers are merely implements of your trade.

Then reread your own managerial job description. Nowhere does it demand or even recommend that you must be human.

CHAPTER 14

Taking
the company line

or

How to tell the employees the complete
and unadulterated truth without once biting
the tongue that's in your cheek.

In fulfilling the reason why God put the hit or miss manager on earth—to get his R/P—the executive absolutely
depends on his underlings. He requires their loyalty, their
obedience, and their industry. He gets this by lying to
them.

Show me one other management treatise that has had
the courage to say that. No, they namby-pamby about and
say that the executive must adhere religiously to company
policy. Okay. I say this: weed out the gobbledygook, and
you're lying to your workers.

Consider the following playlet.

THE TIME: *Many years ago, when innocence continued on
a few years past puberty.*
THE PLACE: *The local Lover's Lane in Anytown, USA.*

  *A boy and a girl are in his dad's car. The girl is gazing
  out the windshield, looking at the full moon above. The*

boy is looking at the girl looking at the moon, and trying to see more of her with each glance. They are both nervous neophytes in the world of eroticism but ready to progress.

GIRL. Isn't the moon beautiful?

BOY. *(in a husky voice)* I don't know.

GIRL. It's so romantic up here, but do you think we should be doing this?

BOY. Oh yeah.

GIRL. I've never let a boy touch me like this before.

BOY. Me neither . . . I mean, I've never touched a boy this way . . . I mean a girl this way before.

GIRL. It feels . . . strange. *(He jumps back and gives her a look of panic; she quickly covers.)* But nice . . . very nice.

BOY. I'm glad. I like it too.

GIRL. I don't think you should be putting your hand under my sweater like that.

BOY. I have to. My hands are very cold.

GIRL. They feel warm.

BOY. No, they're cold. I'll just put them under your sweater up here by your back.

GIRL. Why are you squeezing them?

BOY. I'm not squeezing them—oh, you mean my hands. Well, I'm getting cramps.

GIRL. You're trying to unhook my bra.

BOY. Is that what it feels like?

GIRL. Yes, it does.

BOY. No, it doesn't.

GIRL. Yes, it does. I know what it feels like to unhook a bra.

BOY. You gotta let me do it, please. Let me unsnap it, please. I'll put it right back when I'm done.

GIRL. No.

BOY. C'mon, we're old enough.

GIRL. Stop it. You'll break my shoulder blades.

BOY. Please let me unhook it. I'm in no condition to stop now.

GIRL. Do you really love me?

BOY. I love you like crazy.

GIRL. Am I the only one you'll ever love?

BOY. I will never look at another girl as long as I live, I promise.

GIRL. *(demanding)* Cross your heart.

BOY. I don't want to move my hands.

GIRL. Do you still think Mary Adams is prettier than me?

BOY. Mary Adams is a dog. I couldn't look at her without throwing up. You're the only pretty girl in the school.

GIRL. How about Susie Belson?

BOY. Susie Belson is the ugliest girl I ever saw, believe me. How does this thing work?

GIRL. Move your hands. I'll do it myself.

BOY. You're not just trying to get rid of my hands?

GIRL. I'll do it. *(She reaches behind her back, but takes her sweet time with the unharnessing.)* Will you respect me in the morning?

BOY. I'll respect you the whole damn day, honest to God.

GIRL. Will you fight for my affections if you have to?

BOY. I'll take on the whole freaking football team. I'll swim the highest mountains, I'll climb the deepest ocean. I'll do your homework for a year. I thought you knew how to work that thing—what's taking so damn long?

The rest of this play is best left between the two youngsters, but you all know how it goes after this point anyway.

The point that's being made here is that this young male would have said anything for his first caress of bare breast. From the moment he got his hands on those recalcitrant hooks and eyes of his companion's brassiere, nothing that came from his lips was true. He still thinks Mary Adams is gorgeous, and he'll surely try to get Susie Belson to this same location the next time he gets the keys to his dad's car.

Few of us would condemn this lad. He has a goal in sight, and he'll say anything to acquire that forbidden fruit.

As manager, you are often confronted with a similar dilemma. You have to reiterate the company line to the employees when you really don't believe it yourself.

You have to be even more two-faced than the poor lad in our playlet because you must be more cold-blooded. At least this youngster had the excuse that he had lost himself in the frenzy of passion. Not even the most devoted of us can claim an orgasmic affection for company policy.

It is not easy to be this deceitful when in truth you are an honest, sincere, ingenuous individual. Those words of fraudulence are not easily forced out of a body that doesn't feel them; but you need to learn to utter them, with sincerity. You call your employees together and propagandize for the company. Why? Because you have that honorable managerial objective in sight. You want to get ahead. Therefore, you must do the corporation's bidding.

You would not get very far if you rebelled. Not too many

businesses would have promotions in store for the executive who said, "I'm not going to pass any of your baloney on
to the employees because it is all pure poppycock."

Picture how far the high-school boy in our drama would
have gotten if he had replied to the question "Do you love
me?" with "Hell, no. I just want to get your underwear off
and feel your boobs." His date probably would have given
him a black eye, thrown him out of the car, and run him
over with his father's automobile.

Lest you feel guilty about proselytizing for your employers, however, listen to the other side of the story. Do you
honestly believe that the girl in our play gave any credence
whatsoever to what her amateurish paramour was saying?
Did she think her lover would indeed take on the football
team, climb a mountain, or swim an ocean? Hardly. The
klutz couldn't even unsnap a training bra.

She knew it was the teenager's apprentice lust that was
speaking out. So, bury your guilt. Your employees know
what you're doing. They're aware that this is company ven-
triloquism speaking through your wooden jaws. They accept your discourse in much the same way as they receive a
television commercial. Sure, they sit there submissively
and listen to your spiel, but mentally they are out in the
kitchen getting a snack or in the bathroom washing their
hands of you.

Let's pause for a mome
Miss Management's pr

1. Your primar
   career.
2. There i
   When
   coffee
3. Let otl
   your
   labor.

Now so
"There's tl
on others

Why d
Drucker
me had
ten's sa
business

Certa
Do you h

The ones go

a
ex
hall
He
all my
animals
good end
I unco
always bus
they lug th
going into th
they all work
studied them fo
salary schedule
They're crazy little
Any time you see
You'll even notice the
rying the food and the

e wor
ve I see
pool. No
observati
across anyth
nature's grou

your author could not transcend was this very one: You have to get others to do the work for you. Remember our axiom: To get to the top of the heap, first you must have a heap.

The question is not why, where, what, or when, but *how* do you get others to do your work for you? Your author considered this extensively. You should know by now that your author thinks deeply about all matters concerning the executive world. Man, if you don't know that by now, I'm tempted to give you your money back . . . but I won't.

However, I searched for this answer where I searched for many answers—in nature's wonderland. "What do the animals do?" I asked myself. Whatever the animals do is good enough for management.

I discovered an interesting phenomenon. Beavers are busy as . . . well, as beavers. They chew down trees, they haul them through the forest, they get their feet wet in the muddy water, but they build the dam. And they work hard, each doing his or her fair share. I watched for many long hours, and nowhere did I find a boss for any beaver. They do all this work with a will. They don't even merit a two-week vacation. Busy rodents.

I watched a family of ants, they are all working. Note there are two lines of ants, the ones carrying and the ones returning to the food source to haul. The ones coming back to work are moving as fast as the ones working. It's almost as if they relish their toil. Never seen an ant lying on his back by the anthill, not alive at any rate.

The examination of our lesser brothers and sisters reveals nothing so much as resembling a boss. Yet their endeavors are fantastically organized, yet there is no animal management. All of the beavers were chopping wood. None were at a meeting. All of the ants were carrying bread. None were carrying briefcases.

The inevitable *Hit or Miss Management* conclusion: work is natural; management is unnatural.

Oh, I know you're going to say that earlier I used the example of the knock-kneed, cross-eyed ram. (Boy, my next book is going to be aimed at a more gullible readership.) Yes, I did hold the ram up as an example, but that was different. He served as the leader of a flock. He was protecting either his young or the mating privileges to the females of the flock. *Hit or Miss Management* would never advocate leaving sex to chance.

Nevertheless, you do not see anyone in nature lording it over the workers, and therefore my observations are valid (*author's raspberry*).

So *Hit or Miss Management* says that in order to manage the workers effectively, just stay the hell out of their way. The most effective management is no management at all. Basically people do want to work. Well, maybe that's too generous a statement, but since they have to be there for eight hours, working makes the time go faster.

If you take a milkman's horse and give him an option, he would just as soon stay in the stable or graze in the fields or possibly even do some stud duty. Most workers would choose any of those options, too. But once you rig the equine up in a harness and attach a cart to his rear end, he figures he might as well pull the damn cart and get home as fast as he can.

Employees likewise know that they are in their figurative harness for those eight hours a day. They might as well get their work done and get on home.

Present-day management tries to force or cajole people into working. That it is unnatural and ineffective is proven by our lousy productivity. Following the theorists, management has tried threats, bribes, inspiration, and motivation, but all of these attempts have only succeeded in getting business to the point we are at today.

The organic system is superior. No beaver-built dam has had to be recalled because of poor workmanship and no ant farm has ever been shut down because of labor problems.

The current erroneous management procedures have screwed up the natural system to such an extent that the workers react inorganically. Can I tell you how to handle this problem? Certainly, but quit rushing my writing. I only have ten fingers. (Geez!) It's in the next chapter.

CHAPTER 16

People problems

or
Gepetto was a happy man
when Pinocchio was just a dummy.

What is management? Is it figures, sales projections, quotas, and the like? It is not. It's getting the product out the back door. When the merchandise gets shipped to the customer and the customer sends a check back, then you've "done business."

In order to get a product out the back door, someone has to put the nails in the shipping crate. Who does that? A person. If you've got a lot of persons banging nails, that amounts to people, and that's what management is about—people.

However, people generate problems, and problems can keep you from getting that next, all-important R/P. To get that you must solve those problems as they arise.

In the next few pages I've listed some of the more common office disturbances that an executive might encounter on the way up the management mountain. Learn how to deal with them as creatively and effectively as I have, and you'll be well on your way to the top.

113

The Rubber Band Fight

Case History No. 57968

This happened to me in one of my early supervisorial assignments. I headed a group of some thirty-five draftsmen and drafting apprentices, who would spend a goodly portion of the working day having rubber-band fights. Costs were up, and productivity was low. More importantly (much more importantly), my job was in jeopardy.

When not engaged in actual combat, they would practice incessantly, knocking over pencil holders, killing flies, and stinging any employee who would bend over. At the end of the workday there were rubber bands all over the floor.

I didn't need charts and cost analyses to know that this was wasting valuable working time and costing a small fortune in supplies. While they were supposed to be working for me, my charges were reenacting the Battle of the Bulge, and I was buying the ammunition.

My first move was to assemble the warriors and give them a little talking to.

"My beloved industrial archers," I began. (A little bit of lighthearted humor, but they knew what I was talking about.) "It looks like the Goodyear blimp exploded in this place. The janitor is complaining that he can't sweep the floors in the evening because every time he pushes the broom, it bounces back in his face."

Now my little bit of comedy had caught their attention. I detailed what their military games were costing the department in both time and materials. More importantly, I stressed the safety factor. I ended my speech with a fist-pounding pronouncement: "There will be no more rubber-band shooting in this place of business."

Then I didn't make another move for three weeks. It took that long for the welt marks to go away.

This was early in my career, and I hadn't yet learned that when distressing situations erupt, they are rarely quelled with words, no matter how eloquent the speaker. (And you must admit, I was pretty damn eloquent.)

I didn't need a graphic slide show to convince me, while I was getting stung by 400 angry rubber bands, that my talk was ineffective. I sensed that intuitively.

I rationed rubber bands. You got a rubber band when you needed a rubber band—no more, no less. I didn't want to be tyrannical and deprive working draftsmen of the rubber bands necessary for the completion of their assigned duties. However, I was determined to make them in short supply. I wanted them to become so precious that no one would dare waste one on an act of aggression against a fellow worker.

If a worker wanted one, he simply filled out a requisition form and submitted it to the drafting department secretary, who immediately made several copies. One went into the file, and one came to my desk, and a third copy was delivered to the supply room, where an order form was made out in triplicate. The yellow copy of this went to the supervisor in charge, the green went into the file, and the pink went to the supply clerk who would then get the rubber band from the supply bin and attach it to the pink copy. All of these requested rubber bands were picked up and delivered back to the drafting office by a mail clerk. The secretary would then check them against the request forms and deliver them to the requester, who would sign the receipt form, which was then Xeroxed so that a copy could be presented to my desk and another copy returned to the files of both the mail room and the supply room.

This system didn't work either. Why? I'll tell you why. Because I made a classic youthful management error. I acted against the system and not against the perpetrators of the offense. In spite of my efforts, they got all the rubber bands they wanted. From where, I have no idea, and I was not about to stand in front of that group once more and ask.

Today's manager would have fired a few expendable scapegoats and wasted several hundred hours drawing up diagrams and schedules to prove that the previous failures weren't his fault. But I knew better.

They *were* my fault. A hit or miss manager hits or misses. I simply hadn't been aggressive enough. I was determined that plan three would be vigorous, purposeful, and effective.

This plan took some thought and much evening work on my part. Simple but brilliant, it was based solely on sabotage. I just removed the firing pins from their rubber bands.

That's right. After work each night I would stay in the office. I went through each desk and cut a slit in every rubber band I found.

The next day, when my hapless employees took aim and stretched their weapons back until they reached their breaking points, the bands snapped in half and hit them in their mischievous little noses.

Good for them! And I was serenely innocent. No court can object to corporal discipline if it is self-administered.

There was much weeping and gnashing of teeth—except from my own office, of course, from which only a delighted giggle of victory could be heard.

The moral of this little tale is: If any of your underlings threaten your next R/P, bodily harm is an acceptable deterrent. My mom told me years ago the best way to keep the cat off the couch was to allow the dog on it.

The Air-Conditioning Dilemma

Case History No. 59777

There are hundreds of stories about air conditioners in business. This is one of them. It happened to me in Philadelphia when I managed a roomful of key-punch operators. If you think you're going to learn how to solve the problem of controlling the temperature in a business office, though, don't get your hopes up. That problem is unresolvable. But I did solve *my* problem by keeping them from bugging me further about it. (Some solutions are only partial.)

As I mentioned before, I've always told my employees that they could ask me any question at any time. It's no big deal, because if I don't have the answer, I give them one anyway.

Now be careful, because this is not the same as that old management cliché, "My door is always open." I made the mistake of trying that one in my early years, and the employees took advantage of it. They threw in stink bombs, what was left of their lunches, little doggie do-dos they bought at the joke store, and some they didn't. It was enough to convince me that my door was not always open anymore.

Anyway, back to the case history. My key-punch operators divided themselves into two groups. One group always complained that the office was too hot, and they would turn the thermostat down. The others protested that the room was too cold, and—you guessed it—they would turn the thermostat up. I called them my "hotties" and "coldies," and they made the Hatfields and the McCoys look like they were having a love affair.

At first I tried to stay out of it. I remained in my office with my individual thermostat set the way I like it. That they couldn't stand, so they sent their shop steward in to see me.

I knew that if I gave in to the shop steward for the coldies, the hotties would dispatch their representative in with their complaints, and I'd quickly become the Ping-Pong ball between two merciless union paddles.

The bothersome employees thought they had me on the horns of a dilemma. They were wrong, since they had not encountered as Solomonlike a mind as mine before.

I calmly answered both groups' grievances the same way. I told them the temperature alternated between hot and cold because the building was having a change of life.

The moral of this story is this: The truth will never hurt you, but sometimes a good lie can really help.

Office Collections

Case History No. 60013

A favorite nonproductive pastime for the nonworking worker is the office collection, all the more insidious because it appears to be for a good cause.

Many of these ventures are indeed charitable and commendable. Most of them, however, are just another way of getting out of work. I often wonder how much the beneficiaries would receive if the collections were taken up on the employees' own time.

Do you realize that in many companies across the nation the employees annually collect amounts higher than the net revenues of the businesses? That's right. Many corporations would be well advised to cease their main business and simply settle for a percentage of the take. It works in Las Vegas, so why not in business?

The collectors have a way of allowing these things to grow. As collections become more complex, two or three employees are occupied drawing the get-well card, another one or two are gathering signatures, and so forth. Properly organized, a good collection can paralyze an office routine totally.

When I rose to a position of some authority, my first response was to ban from the office any activity that would result in a collection having to be taken up. Attack the problem at its source. Remove all temptation and sin becomes obsolete. So I wrote the following letter:

Dear Employees:
There are some extracurricular activities that are
affecting the efficient operation of the office in which

we all work. Since it is to the benefit of all of us to
maintain this business on a profit-making basis, the
following activities are hereby banned from this place of
employment:

1. Illness of any consequence.
2. Bearing children.
3. Allowing pets to bear children.
4. Reaching the age of sixty-five.
5. Leaving this employment to enter military service
   or to go to any other place of employment.
6. Graduating from college, high school, high-school
   equivalency, trade school, or school of any kind.
7. Permitting children or relatives of any kind to
   graduate from institutions mentioned in point
   six.
8. Dying.
9. Permitting relatives or pets to engage in activity
   described in point eight.
10. Any other activity and/or occasion that might
    result in a gift being given by your fellow workers.

I would appeal to your common business sense to
adhere to the above regulations.

> Yours truly,
> The Manager

The letter was a mistake. I knew I had made an error.
The union committee knew it was not right. The court that
eventually tried the case was manifest in its belief that I was
wrong.

Fortunately, my employees took up a collection to help
pay a portion of the fine.

I was grateful for that, but nothing could dissuade me
from my objective.

The solution to the problem turned out to be much sim-
pler than I had expected. It was simply to use what I call

"managerial jiujitsu," another phrase you won't find in other management books. Jiujitsu is the art of using an opponent's force against him. It explains why a smaller person can throw a much larger adversary to the ground. For example, if a huge person comes at you, instead of trying to resist his bulk, you flow with his motion, roll along with it, and act as a lever, allowing the person's force and momentum to carry him in the direction you want him to go.

In most offices it's obvious that there is a ringleader of office collections, a sort of Al Capone of the cigar box. He or she will collect for the most minor of occasions. So far I had donated to dog matings and helped defray the cost of burying hamsters. Using our collection head's own enthusiasm against him was the jiujitsu thing to do.

I made office collections official company policy. That immediately turned the average worker against it. Then I attacked the ringleader and made office collections part of his job description. Now he never does it.

Office Gambling

Case History No. 60121

Breathes there an office worker with soul so dead, who never to himself has said, "Let's see, should I pick the Vikings over the Rams or the Cardinals over the Eagles?" Football pools are probably the only thing in offices all over the nation that are completed on schedule.

Office workers get bored with not working, so they turn to gambling. Idle hands are the bookie's workshop. They gamble on everything. Even as they take up a collection for a person who is out with a lengthy illness, they throw in an extra quarter and have a pool on which day their coworker will return to the office.

The morality and the legality of the gambling didn't concern me. I gave the workers their paychecks, and what they did with them after that concerned me not at all. However, all of the planning, the collecting, the meditating on who will win on a given Sunday, the payoffs, and the discussions about how close one came to winning—all this was done on my time. I was paying cold cash, sometimes with a cost-of-living escalation clause, for their little diversions. The boss is the only one who loses no matter who wins or how much is won.

It doesn't take too much smarts to realize that this kind of thing has to be ended in an office. I decided to act with determination and expedition. I called all my gamblers together. Then I came out of my office ranting and raving about the time and money that was being wasted and issued a clear and forceful ultimatum: there would be no more gambling during business hours. After a moment of silence, one employee walked over to another and handed over a fistful of money. They had a pool going about when I would come out of my office ranting and raving about the time and money that was being wasted on gambling.

The hit or miss manager is not dissuaded by failure. Next I took more drastic measures. For the good of the company and the efficiency of the operation, I turned stoolie. That's right. I ratted to the authorities. Gambling is illegal, and in the business world we don't want any illegalities to exist except those necessary for conducting the business. I had our office raided.

Twenty-eight of my workers were arrested and charged with gambling, which didn't please me at all. I had twenty-six in the pool.

Tardiness

Case History No. 61178

I like my employees to be at their desks and ready to begin work when the starting bell rings. I'm a stickler for that. In fact, that's the first thing I ask my secretary when I get to my office: "How many of the workers were here on time?"

My workday always began at nine o'clock sharp. A certain number of employees never got there before 9:10. If the workday began at 9:10, they would get there at 9:20. If the workday began at ten o'clock, they would get there at . . . you guessed it. If the workday began at midnight, they would get there at midnight:10. At the end of the world, these people will be ten minutes late and won't know what the hell happened.

I've talked to some of these ten-minuters. One gentleman told me he had tried everything. He had attempted driving a different route to work. He had searched for a parking place that was nearer to the office. He had even bought a smaller car that might be faster. He tried everything except leaving the house ten minutes earlier. When I suggested that radical alternative to him, he said, "Then who's going to be home to finish my breakfast?"

I suggested to another ten-minuter that she leave the house eleven minutes earlier. She didn't like that because she didn't know what she would do to kill that extra minute before work started.

Almost every talk I gave to my assembled hirelings included a plea for promptness. Each one, no matter how creative and impressive, was rebuffed.

Once I tried to dazzle them with mathematics. I impressed upon them the statistic that 50 percent of them were getting to work fifteen minutes late every morning. I told them, "Very little work gets done in this office between 9:00 and 9:15." The next morning, nobody showed up on time. The 50 percent were still fifteen minutes late, and the rest of them figured that if there was so little going on, they might as well catch a little extra sleep, too.

Hit or Miss Management teaches that if at first you don't succeed, go ahead and give it another shot. I appealed to their sense of fair play. I explained the complicated machinations that we executives go through to arrive at an equitable salary system. The money we pay them is based on a formula that is dependent on the amount of work they do in return. The amount of work they do is in turn formulated according to the number of hours they will be in the office. Ergo, when they are not in the office, it throws off the calculations and eats into the company's profits. Boiling it all down to simplistic terms for their consideration, I said, "Coming to work late is like stealing money from the company." The next day the same number came in late, but they all wore stockings over their faces.

I abandoned all efforts to relate their lateness to the company. No soft spot existed in their hearts for the hand that fed them. This time, history was my focal point. I called a 9:30 meeting because I wanted to start no later than ten o'clock. At 10:10 I began my talk, and the stragglers would just have to miss the beginning of it. In stressing the importance of punctuality, I asked, "Would Wellington have been victorious if he hadn't been on time for Waterloo?" This would give them something to ponder, I thought. They needed no time. One employee responded with, "If Napoleon had been late, Wellington would have had nobody to defeat." The meeting was adjourned.

Now I was getting angry. My next dissertation was downright nasty. I said, "If your wife came into the bedroom two minutes late each time you made love, she'd miss everything." Then some wise guy came back with, "Your wife gets there on time and still misses everything."

In anger, I simply blurted out, "How would you like it if *I* came in late every day?" I guess that finally reached them, because it got a standing ovation.

Now I have abandoned all of this infantile game playing and have adopted a cold-blooded, ruthless attitude toward tardiness. At nine o'clock sharp, the doors to the offices are locked and bolted shut. Should an employee arrive at 9:01, plead and cajole to enter, weep and gnash his or her teeth

—tough noogies. The portals remain unopened. I am happy to say that lateness has been totally eliminated. Oh, attendance is way down, but that's another problem.

Using the Telephone for Personal Calls

Case History No. (well, this is not so much a case history as a continuing battle)

Every business office has a telephone, and every office has telephone users. What every office does not have is a guarantee that the person on the phone is engaged in enhancing the company's position in the marketplace.

Most people are calling to line up a date for tonight or to find out the lurid details about their friend's date the prior night. Some are calling to make sure that there will be some lurid details on their own date for tonight. Some talk food, some sex, some sports. Some lucky ones discuss a combination of the three. Others telephone to find out if their canary is still shaking on the floor of the cage. There are about as many reasons for calling as there are combinations of numbers on the dial.

Only about 2 percent of all telephone usage has anything to do with the company, and even that is permitted by the employees only grudgingly.

"Hey, Charlie, this call's for you. Some guy wants to purchase $200,000 worth of merchandise or something. Hurry up with it, willya. I gotta call the wife and see if the puppy peed on the new rug yet today."

I've worked in places where if the building caught fire, we'd have to summon the fire department by a special-delivery letter.

The hit or miss manager knows this has to be stamped out. It is expensive, it's a terrible waste of time, and it can raise your blood pressure more than a surprise visit from government auditors. Instead of chatting whimsically on the phone, the little darlings should be busting their tails trying to get you that next R/P.

I have waged war against this infraction throughout my brilliant career. First I pleaded with my underlings to desist. We've noticed before that pleading is generally fruitless. All they did was rush to the phone to call their friends and joke about how ludicrous my efforts were.

His or Miss Management accepts failure as a reality and moves on to the next, more aggressive step. I typed this official, severely worded memo.

MEMO:
TO: All employees of Eugene R. Perret
FROM: Eugene R. Perret, manager
SUBJECT: Use of the company telephones for personal calls.

HEY! Stop using the company phones for personal calls. Okay?

I then had my secretary post this firm admonition on all the bulletin boards. This worked no better than the talk had. No one ever reads the company bulletin boards. In a business office, should you commit a murder and want to hide the body, tack it to the bulletin board.

A second failure does not deter the hit or miss manager; in fact, my students are used to it. Next, I acted even more dynamically. I had locks installed on all the phones. This was the moment when I discovered a strange phenomenon that exists only in business offices: locks cease to function. Should one of your employees be out sick and important documents are locked in her desk, her fellow employees can retrieve them as if they were in an open field. Folders disappear from locked filing cabinets, and remnants of sloppy lunches are found in locked conference rooms. I have even arrived in the morning, unlocked my private office, opened the lock I had installed on my private telephone, picked up the receiver, and found it was still warm.

My hit or miss management mind persisted despite many defeats. This time my plan of attack was to use embarrassment. I hooked all the phones to public speakers. Every conversation was broadcast to the entire work force. I liked this idea. The employees did not. The unions did not. The American Civil Liberties Union did not. The judge who tried the case did not. After the sentence was handed down, even I did not.

And so the battle continues. The statement I'm about to make is astounding. You will never read it in any of Druck's books, nor McGregor's, nor Townsend's. Only the author of *Hit or Miss Management* has the courage and the humility to make this statement.

I have not found an answer to this problem.

That's right, beloved readers, there does exist a problem that has temporarily defeated the inventiveness of the father of *Hit or Miss Management*.

Therefore, I challenge you, the newest disciples of hit or miss management, to come up with solutions to this telephonic transgression. Send your solutions to me, and the one that is most inventive and most practical will be richly rewarded: I will have lunch with the winner. Of course, transportation costs must be provided by you, but we will go Dutch on the lunch.

All you need do is write out your solution in English (I've been too busy studying managerial procedures to become much of a linguist) and send it to me along with a receipt for the book or the convenient proof-of-purchase seal on the inside of the jacket. I want to be sure that you bought the book. After all, why should I have lunch with a deadbeat?

Dressing Too Sexily

Every office has one woman who dresses like a hooker. I do know it occurs periodically in a business office, and without being moralistic about this problem it's wrong for the office. It causes work stoppages in too many ways. Guys can't work when they stop to stare. No one can contribute an effective eight hours of labor without blinking. Women can't work when they stop to whisper. No one can be productive for the full day without taking a breath. Men who work near our sexy offender are constantly dropping their pencils, just so they can bend over to pick them up and sneak a quick glance.

All of these realities must be pointed out to this woman, who actually may be unaware of the commotion she is causing.

In this situation what I generally do is invite her into my office, have a few drinks, and talk the problem over. Sometimes just pointing out the distractions they are causing is enough to terminate the problem. That's what happened in this case.

Case History No. 78927

I called Miss X (to protect her privacy, I will not use her last name) into my private office for a talk.

She entered wearing a very low-cut V-neck dress, cut all the way down to the fire-engine-red belt that encircled her deliciously tiny waist. Her skirt was tight and short, and her legs were tight and long. She wore very high-heeled shoes. I was very glad we had decided to have this little talk.

TRIXIE. You wanted to see me, Mr. Perret?

ME. Yes. Come in please, Trixie. Close that door behind you, would you, please?

TRIXIE. Certainly.

(She has a cute way of saying that so that it sounded more like "Soitenly." It is hard for her to enunciate with the gum she is chewing.)

ME. Sit down, my dear.

TRIXIE. Okay.

(She sits across the desk from me.)

ME. Now I want you to relax, Trixie.

TRIXIE. Okay.

ME. You don't have to sit all the way over there. Sit over here beside my desk where I can talk to you better.

TRIXIE. Okay.

(She moves to the side of the desk where I can see her better.)

ME. Put your feet up on the desk if you like.

TRIXIE. Naw, this is okay.

ME. You're welcome to.

TRIXIE. Naw.

ME. Please.

TRIXIE. What?

ME. I mean, if you please, we can get started.

TRIXIE. Okay.

ME. Now, Trixie, did you know that the production output of the people working around you is 14.72 percent lower than the average output of the entire office?

TRIXIE. No.

ME. Look here at these figures on my desk.

(She rises and glances at them.)

ME. You should really see these figures, Trixie. Bend way over and look at them.

(She does.)

TRIXIE. I don't know what they mean.

ME. That's because you're not looking closely enough. Bend way over.

TRIXIE. *(bending way over my desk)* Like that?

ME. Ooohh, perfect.

TRIXIE. I don't see anything that has to do with me.

ME. I do.

TRIXIE. What?

ME. Uh . . . I do, because I'm more experienced at reading these complicated figures than you are.

TRIXIE. Oh.

ME. The production rate in your vicinity is only 38.53 units.

TRIXIE. Is that bad?

ME. Well, let's just compare it to the production rate of, say, 1912.

TRIXIE. 1912?

ME. Yes, would you get that volume for me? It's way on the top shelf. You can stand on that chair.

TRIXIE. Okay. *(She begins to climb up on the chair and reach for the volume.)* I'm a little scared. This chair is shaky.

ME. Here, I'll hold you.

(I reach up and hold onto parts of her solicitously.)

Now that's as much as I remember of this case history. I blacked out at that moment and woke up with a terrible knot on my head. The company physician said it looked like

I had been hit with the 1912 output production volume.
The poor girl must have been so frightened she dropped it
on my skull.

But the point was made. Miss X was so embarrassed at
the figures I exposed to her that she never showed up in
that office again. I'm certain she realized that her attire was
a detriment to my managerial goals and she chose to leave
rather than jeopardize my advancement . . . no matter
what her lawyer said in his subsequent letter.

CHAPTER 17

Cutting costs

or
Anything that's worth doing
is worth doing well—unless it's
cheaper to do it pretty good.

From the employer's point of view, the manager's only reason for being on the payroll is to make money for the company. We've already seen that the manager's first priority is to make money for himself. It would seem that these two goals are in opposition. In fact, however, they are perfectly complementary.

The more money a manager saves the company, the better he looks in the eyes of that company. The more money the corporation has available for raises, the more promotions they can hand out. Naturally, they will hand them out to those people who look good in their eyes—namely, the manager who saved them the money in the first place. Consequently, it behooves you to save them some money.

The only pitfall might be if you save them so much money that they can afford to hire somebody who's better qualified than you and who can save them even more money.

Peter Drucker, in his well-respected (though I'll never know why) *Managing for Results*, tells us that "costs—their identification, measurement, and control—are the most thoroughly worked, if not overworked, business area. An enormous amount of work goes into cost control, an enormous amount of time goes to cost analysis."

Now all of this nonsense costs money, *and* it does no good. We all know that costs go up every year, always have, always will, forever and ever. Amen.

Druck himself admits this. Three valuable pages of his book are spent conceding this very point, after which he finally offers us his sage advice. He says, "To be able to control costs, a business therefore needs a cost analysis which . . . ," then he lists five irrelevant points. Such contradiction needs no further discussion.

Hit or Miss Management says: If you're going to analyze, you're going to spend; if you're going to cut costs, cut them and don't fool around.

Where can a hit or miss manager best attack in his cost-reduction war? He is in no position to reduce salaries, because they are set by people at the corporate level. Can he attack the cost of materials? No. These are generally determined by a group of whimsical foreigners who inherited an oil well, copper mine, or coffee bush from their forerunners.

The biggest item of expenditure within the manager's control is toys. That's right—TOYS—for his employees.

The darlings can't be expected to sit there and work for a full eight hours each and every day, five days a week, so they play little games to keep their minds occupied. They keep their tiny hands busy with the clever games they make up from the odds and ends they find in the supply cabinet.

A goodly part of the manager's hard-won budget goes toward those provisions that keep the wheels of industry grinding, but very few employees are concerned about that. They see our precious stationery provisions as nothing more than common, ordinary playthings.

We've already seen what can happen when an innocent rubber band gets into the hands of our fun-loving pranksters. Here are a few other problems I've encountered along the same lines.

Paper Clips

Some day I would like to find the person who invented the paper clip, chain him to a post with his own invention, and give him forty lashes with a No. 5 rubber band.

This is not an attack on the man's ingenuity; no one can deny his inventiveness. I'm amazed that he could have sat up one night and discovered that you can take a piece of wire, bend it into an intriguing shape, and create a device that will hold several pieces of paper together. When finished, he probably trudged smugly off to bed with no thought to the problems he had created. He should have foreseen the myriad of other uses to which his devilish little patent could be put.

For example, the contrivance fairly demands to be made into a chain. Now, a simple chain of paper clips is not a nuisance in itself, but it creates a competitive atmosphere among the workers that can become quite costly. Each department wants to be the proud owner of the longest chain in the office.

This kind of perversion goes on endlessly—literally endlessly, because another property of the demonic wire device is that it has no end. There's never been a paper-clip chain that does not have room for one more clip.

Besides the cost of the multitudinous links in the chains, which, incidentally, have no function (this is another quarrel I have with the originator, why create something that begs to be linked to its own kind, but once linked becomes totally ineffective for the purpose for which it was originally designed?), there is also the cost of the man-hours expended in linking the wiry little devils together.

There is another type of paper-clip chain that is even more costly as far as labor goes because of the clandestine nature of its manufacture. This is the trick chain. One employee is chosen as the victim, and the others secretly try to link her supply of paper clips together without being discovered. It is quite a coup in some offices to link a coworker's entire supply together. Then, of course, there is great hilarity when she reaches in her drawer for a paper clip and pulls out some 642, all linked together in unbroken succession. It's terribly amusing to the idle workers, but not at all funny to the manager who pays for the clips, the labor of uniting them, and the time required for the victim to angrily disconnect the links.

I personally hate the little gadgets. I once thought of running for political office just so I could sponsor the "Use a paper clip, go to jail" bill.

Some youngsters work in an office for two or three months before they discover that the paper clip was made to hold pieces of paper together. They think it was actually designed for the innumerable other functions they see it serve during the course of a day. It is shot from rubber bands at unsuspecting coworkers. It is used to clean lord knows how many ears. It is used as an instrument of sabotage to clog the copying machine. It's a kind of Tinker Toy for bored workers who enjoy bending it into varied and interesting shapes.

To deal with this insidious problem, I simply ban the use of paper clips in any office that I'm in charge of. The staple is much preferred for the simple reason that until it is put into use, it is safely hidden inside a machine, far away from curious and idle hands.

Pencils

If you equated it to human terms, the average life expectancy of the office pencil would be about thirteen years. Very few of them are productive to maturity, however. They are thrown away in anger, broken for the sake of a joke, lost, or used to stir coffee and then discarded (few office pencils can survive being dipped in office coffee). Even in their short life span, they are used for purposes other than those for which they were designed. They are sharpened about two or three times and functional no more.

In one place where I worked, we even had an office puzzle, riddle, or trick, whatever you want to call it (I know what I called it). A person would break a pencil with a dollar bill. The trick was passed along from one friend to another, shattered pencils scattered in their wake. It irritated me, first, because no one ever taught me how to do it, and, second, because I was paying for it. It was bad enough when I was paying for an entire pencil and getting only about a 10 percent efficiency rate, but now this saloon game was decimating even my productive writing implements.

I've since adopted the philosophy of the bartender who demands to see the empties before opening a new bottle. I demand a stub that can no longer be grasped between the first finger and thumb before I issue a new No. 2.

I give my stationery clerks firm orders that they are only to accept a pencil that is totally ungraspable, worn down to the very metal that holds the eraser in place, before they issue a new writing instrument.

I don't want them to rush ahead and hand out pencils until the employees start getting on the ball and using theirs fully, so the catch phrase in my stationery-supply office is, "Don't get the lead out and hand the lead out until the workers get the lead out and start getting the lead out."

Paper

Paper is another large and unnecessary expenditure in almost all offices. Every worker should have something to write on, but the privilege is abused.

If I had my way, every office would come equipped with a palimpsest. Look it up in a dictionary and see if you don't agree with me. I was right, wasn't I?

People do a few figures on a large sheet of paper, get their answer, then tear off the sheet and throw it away. Only about 3 percent of the writing surface has been used, yet the entire piece of paper is thrown out—both sides.

If you took all the scratch paper that is used on a typical day in our office and laid it end to end, it would cover the entire state of Pennsylvania. The part that was written on, however, would barely cover Betsy Ross's house.

Copying Machines

The photostatic copier is probably the most expensive item in the whole industrial-toy catalog. Paper shoots out of this thing as if the mechanical monster had manuscript diarrhea.

One has to wonder what on earth we did before this machine was devised. Certainly we didn't run our offices like the monks of old and copy everything by hand. It's baffling, but we did manage to get our work done without making a copy of everything.

Besides the legitimate copying, which is still largely unnecessary, there is also the problem of recreational reproduction. Private studies have shown that 72.6 percent of all duplicating in an office is done for decorative purposes. Employees print signs, slogans, and jokes with which they beautify their work areas, drawing boards, and bulletin boards.

The person who invented the photostatic copying machine showed the same selfishness as the inventor of the paper clip. Invent the machine, collect the money, and screw all the problems it can create.

For a start, the creator of the machine should also have given mathematics courses to all those who use the invention. The following conversation is a verbatim transcript from my copious files.

WORKER NO. 1. *(to Worker No. 2)* You'd better get me some copies of this.

WORKER NO. 2. *(accepting the sheet of paper)* Okay. How many will you need?

WORKER NO. 1. Let's see. One for the file, one for me, and one for the manager. Eight copies.

Now one plus one plus one equals three. It always has. It always will. One plus one plus one does not equal eight. The inventor of the copier should have mentioned this in the instruction booklet.

He should also have made a slot on the monster that would accept vitamin pills, because the damn thing always requires an X.D.—a doctor of Xerography. There is nearly always someone with a big black case standing next to our machine, removing organs from its exposed bowels. At least he could have made it similar to the horse, so that when it breaks down it could be shot.

Presently I employ a combination copying machine and tape player. When the print button is pushed on the copier, it activates a tape recording of my voice saying, "I see what you're doing. STOP IT."

CHAPTER 18

Hiring

or
Hiring the wrong people is like
having measles. Once you've got them, all
you can do is give them to somebody else.

Drucker and those of his ilk are of no help in this area because, as we've already seen, they don't even admit they have people working for them. They content themselves with "Revenues, Resources, and Prospects" and "Cost Centers and Cost Structures" and "Building Economic Performance into a Business." They must figure that at night, when the plant is closed, tiny leprechauns come in and tippy-tap-tap the product into existence.

If you went to any one of these management theory giants and insisted that you had to hire people to get your work done, they would reply, "What do you have to hire people for? You've got your organizational charts, haven't you?"

Hit or Miss Management is more realistic. It recognizes that you have to hire people, but it admits that you can never know just what you are hiring. Science has yet to devise a mechanism or refine a computer that can supply this kind of information.

In spite of this, you will conduct job interviews because they will be required by your boss, at least until that glori-

138

ous day when all of upper management is converted to the *Hit or Miss Management* system.

The only advice I can give you is this: Have fun with them. You might as well, because you know damn right well that neither you nor the applicant will be telling the truth. So go through the job interview. They're as much fun as having your picture taken with a celebrity, and just about as useful.

Following is a typical job-applicant inquisition that I, the father of *Hit or Miss Management*, conducted.

SETTING: My office. There is a knock at the door, and the applicant enters. He is about six foot three, the upper three inches being hair. He is dressed in jeans and a T-shirt reading "Acapulco Gold." I take this to be his alma mater and the school colors. In his right ear is an earring, and in his left ear are two earrings.

ME. Come in, son.

(He does and hands me his job application.)

ME. *(putting him at his ease)* Is this your job application?

HIM. *(putting me at my ease)* No, man. I'm Blackbeard the Pirate, and that's the map to my hidden treasure.

ME. I see. Well, sit down and relax.

(He does, putting both feet on my desk. I notice he needs the job badly because the yellow sock is neat, but the blue one is kind of ratty.) Were there no ball-point pens in the outer office?

HIM. Oh yeah, man, but I always write with crayon.

ME. Well, let's just take a closer look at this. *(reading)* Um hmmm . . . um hmmmm. Well now, here where it asks you to write your name, we wanted you to put your last name first, your first name last, and your middle initial after everything else.

HIM. Why?

ME. I think it's for filing purposes. You know, so we can look up your last name first.

HIM. Oh. Well, I just put down "Moose" because that's what everybody calls me anyway.

ME. Oh, that's what that is, huh? Moose.

HIM. Yeah, I don't know how to spell it, so I just draw the picture.

ME. Okay, then we'll just file that under "M."

HIM. I guess.

ME. Well, what kind of a job are you applying for?

HIM. I don't know, you know, but I'm kind of good with tools.

ME. Well, I can see that by the way you're cleaning your fingernails with that switchblade knife.

HIM. Thanks, Pal.

ME. Well, let's see what we have available.

(He suddenly leans over my desk.)

HIM. Hey, man, who is that?

ME. Oh, that's a picture of my lovely wife.

HIM. She's gorgeous, Ace. I'd like to see her with no clothes on.

ME. Well, the kids are in the picture and all.

HIM. Hey, do you bring her to the company Christmas party?

ME. Yes, in fact, I do.

HIM. Then I'll take any job you got, man.

ME. Well, you're certainly easy to please. Now do you have any questions?

HIM. Just one. Do you pay sick leave for psychiatric care?

I hired this gentleman. He left my office and reported to the factory foreman. I left the office and reported to the company nurse, who cleaned and bandaged the wound the switchblade had made on my neck. He *was* good with tools.

CHAPTER 19

Firing

or
If thy right hand offends thee, cut it
off—unless it belongs to a strong union.

Terminating employment is a necessary component of the business jungle. It is known by many different euphemisms—cleaning out the deadwood, getting in some new blood, and so forth. And it does serve a purpose of sorts. Lawns do have to be weeded, trees do have to be pruned, toenails do have to be clipped.

Hit or Miss Management is formulated from nature, and none of nature's rules is as readily apparent and as inviolable as this one. All living creatures gracefully accept its inevitability. I'm sure when a field mouse is captured in the viselike talons of the hawk, he would like to glance upwards to the eyes of his predator and say, "Hey, nice catch."

Only the working person rebels against this inescapable reality. Nowhere in nature is there any rule that dictates that animals must be hunted in the order of their seniority. No, the hungry hunters chase and capture the weakest or the slowest of the herd.

Can you imagine the confusion that would result in the animal kingdom if those creatures that are traditionally attacked by their more predatorially inclined compeers joined together to form the Amalgamated Federation of Preyed-upon Animals (AFPUA)?

Consider it.

SETTING: *Somewhere in the jungle. Two leopards are on the hunt. We'll call them Lee and Lester. They approach a herd of grazing antelopes.*

LEE. Yo, Lester. Look at this—a herd of antelopes. Oh man, I think I've died and gone to leopard heaven.

LESTER. They do look scrumptious. And I'm having a big lunch because I'm skipping dinner tonight to hang around the old watering hole.

LEE. I'd say that one over there with the weak-looking antlers is probably our best bet . . . unless you're not in a hurry?

LESTER. Well, we'd better take it easy, Lee. I think this is a union shop.

(There is a stirring in the bush behind them.)

ANDREW. You're damn right it is, gentlemen.

LEE. What the . . . ?

LESTER. Who are you?

ANDREW. *(setting down his imitation-leather briefcase)* I'm Andrew T. Antelope, field representative for the antelope union.

LEE. You're from AFPUA?

ANDREW. That's right. And you two gentlemen seem intent on thinning out the numbers of this particular herd.

LESTER. Yeah, we're kind of hungry.

ANDREW. That's reasonable, and our union has no quarrel with that. Are you signatories to our guild?

LEE. Well, no . . .

ANDREW. In that case, I propose that you sign immediately, or you'll never hunt in this jungle again.

LESTER. What does that mean?

ANDREW. It's all spelled out in this little booklet, but basically it means that you agree to hunt only from member herds, that you attack in a strict order of seniority, that there will be no initiation of any attack that will end in a capture on either a Sunday or an observed holiday, and that any capture occurring on a Saturday or after the close of the normal grazing day must involve an animal and a half.

LESTER. That's crazy, man.

LEE. Yeah, we're not signing that.

ANDREW. All right. (*authoritatively snapping his briefcase shut*) You've asked for a strike. These antelopes are walking.

(*Andrew storms out, the antelope herd marches around in a circle, carrying picket signs, and the leopards are as confused as some of my readers must be by now.*)

It does appear ludicrous, doesn't it? That's because it's unnatural. And yet we in the business world act out this scene every day. *Hit or Miss Management* says that terminations are natural. Keep in mind that all good things must come to an end, and all bad things must be fired.

It is never a pleasant task, but the corporate logic is that if someone is not performing, he is hurting the operation. He is harming not only management but also his fellow workers. He must be removed. Of course, upper management is not really worried that this rotten apple will endanger the other apples. What they're concerned with is the damn barrel.

Nevertheless, the burden of discharging the employee falls on the manager. The bureaucratic powers say that this employee is an inflamed appendix causing pain to the corporate tummy. He is a gallstone that irritates the lining of a particular department. The manager is appointed as the surgeon who must remove this offending organ.

The only problem is that no one has ever invented an effective anesthetic for firing people. That meeting when you call someone into your office to be terminated takes on a funereal cast. Naturally, you would like to break the news to the victim as tactfully as possible, but you can't always soften the blow because the doleful look in your visage betrays your mission.

Naturally, the terminatee is also mournful—*he* is about to be fired. There is a certain permanence to the act that resembles death. The angel of severance is about to strike him down, and he must go through the purgatory of the unemployment line and eventually be committed to the hell of working for another corporation.

He has failed as an employee, and, in a sense, you have failed as a manager. It is fitting that the meeting should take on sepulchral overtones. You, as the still-employed manager, should sympathize with and respect the feelings of the nearly departed. Your mood should remain somber and sedate. Your demeanor should be that of a friend of the bereaved. This is not always easy, as sometimes you're so glad to be getting rid of the turkey that you are laughing hysterically on the inside.

Despite your glee, try to be as humane as possible. You can surely take away a person's employment, but allow him to keep his dignity. Convince him that this move is for his own good and for the good of the company. Assure him that the termination is not because he is inherently a bad worker, but simply because he didn't fit into the company's game plan. Point out that many professional athletes are cut from the roster of one team only to go on to greater heroics with another. Persuade him that as painful as this may seem now, he undoubtedly will move on to bigger and better things. This is not only for his consolation, but for your own satisfaction as well, because if he's clunker enough to buy all this crap, he deserves to be fired.

I myself always try to begin these awkward meetings with a simple joke. This is purely a protective device. It's not at all meant to cheer up the employee; it's my own safety valve. If the laughter that is churning inside of me suddenly bursts forth, I simply tell the poor unfortunate that I'm still laughing at my own joke.

Let me again illustrate with a transcript from one of my (father of *Hit or Miss Management*) severance conferences. On this occasion I had to terminate a worker named Moose. The more alert readers will remember that he was hired in our previous chapter. Now he had to be fired for lack of industry, insubordination, assault and battery with a deadly weapon on two of his fellow workers and one of his foremen, and, worst of all, tardiness. (To reiterate, how could I have known from the job interview that he would not have been punctual?)

SETTING: My office four days after the employment interview, including a three-day weekend. Moose enters.

MOOSE. Hey, did you call me up here to hassle me?

ME. No, no, no, no. Calm down, Moose. I called you up here to tell you a little joke.

MOOSE. Is it dirty?

ME. No, in fact, it's quite . . .

MOOSE. Then forget the joke and let's get on with it.

ME. All right . . . uh . . . Moose . . .

MOOSE. Yeah?

ME. I think I have some good news for you, Moose. You'll never have to worry about looking for a parking space around here again.

MOOSE. You crazy? I bring my motorcycle to work and I park it in the guardhouse.

ME. Is there still room for the guard in there?

MOOSE. No, but so what?

ME. So that's not the good news I have for you, then. But you know the way we always have a big party and we say nice things about someone who has been with the company twenty-five years? I'll bet you don't like that kind of stuff, do you?

MOOSE. Naw, I think that stuff is goofy.

ME. Well, I think I've taken care of that for you.

MOOSE. Hey, I took care of that myself. I told everybody if they try to give me a party, I'll break their goddamn arms.

ME. Oh . . . well . . . I know you hate the company logo.

MOOSE. Yeah, I do. That stupid little square with them fairy letters inside it. It looks crappy.

ME. Well, now, I think your problems are over, Moose.

MOOSE. What the hell are you talking about?

(There is a knock at the door.)

ME. Come in.

(They do.)

ME. Moose, you're probably wondering why I've called ten uniformed police officers into my office?

MOOSE. What the f——?

ME. Moose, you're fired.

A final important note. Even though the employees, through the rumor mill, know that the termination is imminent, don't make it official until the very last moment.

Give the victim only enough time to say good-bye to a few friends, and have him out the door before the full realization sets in. You'd be surprised how much you can save in stolen stationery supplies that way.

CHAPTER 20

Dealing
with unions

or
Compared to labor and management, the
Hatfields and the McCoys are kissing cousins.

Hit or Miss Management again slashes new paths through
the executive jungle. None among my writing peers deals
with the subject of unions. We've already seen hundreds of
examples of my fellow managerial authors not admitting to
having employees. So if they formed a union, who would
join it?

Dealing with the union is a unique encounter in the
business world. It's the only confrontation that has no gen-
teel rules governing it.

All other exchanges in business are controlled by the
lines drawn on the organizational chart. If a person's photo-
graph is above yours on the chart and has a line leading to
your likeness, you do what that person says. (Oh, you argue
periodically for appearances' sake, but you do it.) If a line
from your picture leads to a photo below yours, you tell that
party what to do. That's all there is to it, and for the life of
me I don't know how Peter Drucker can write forty-two
books about that.

The union is the one real challenge a manager faces. It's the only fight that isn't fixed. It's a chance for him to test his managerial muscle against a solid opponent.

Be assured, too, that unions are worthy opponents. Establishment managers tend to underrate these adversaries because they comprise "only workers." They think they can handle them easily, but they forget that these guys are not required by some organizational diagram to take a dive.

It is a tough competition against the unions, and *Hit or Miss Management* takes its usual stand: Avoid the confrontation. Why bother fighting? Would you play tennis or golf with someone who doesn't follow the rules? Then why butt heads with these laborers who refuse to accept the current rules of business?

They're an impossible opponent. All they want is a promotion or more money. What kind of a silly philosophy is that for a worker?

Hit or Miss Management says: Keep them mollified.

An infant is a wondrous thing. It's a tiny, helpless creature that comes into this world naked, not knowing anyone or anything. It can speak no languages. It can't dress itself or even move very much. It can't read or write. In fact, it can hardly see. Lifting its head is a struggle, and it takes months for it to learn to roll over or even sit up. Learning to crawl takes even longer, but that doesn't matter because when it crawls, it has no idea where it's going. It doesn't care because it wouldn't know what to do when it got there anyway. What a pitifully helpless incompetent this child is. Yet this infant can get anything it wants.

"Helpless" is a misnomer because this child is fed, clothed, and comforted. It's put safely into bed each evening and is carefully protected from harm during the day. This diminutive citizen is better off than better people.

How does it get all these luxuries when most of us adults have to fend for ourselves? It does so by a very simple but effective means—crying. As the father and chief executive of a family of four children, I can attest to the fact. Crying does get the infant what it wants.

The same is true of labor unions. They, too, cry for everything they want. If they have a need, they become like little children. They bellow away at the tops of their lungs. They throw themselves on the floor, stamp their feet, and hold their breaths until they are blue around the union label. In short, a temper tantrum is their modus operandi.

Is a strike an adult mode of behavior? I think not. I remember a kid, Tommy Mahoney, who lived in my neighborhood when I was a youngster. I hated that kid. He always had to pitch for our baseball team. We never won a game because Tommy was a lousy pitcher. Then why did we consent to have him take the mound for every game? Because he owned the ball. If he didn't get to pitch, he'd take the ball and go home. It was better to lose than not to play at all.

A labor union on strike is doing an impersonation of Tommy Mahoney. They're saying, "We want things our way in this factory, or else we will take our nuts and bolts and go home." And they will, too.

Please don't misconstrue this as a condemnation of labor unions. I would no more condemn them for what they are doing than I would condemn a tiny baby for crying when it is hungry. (I *am* condemning Tommy Mahoney, though.) The baby cries because the reflex is instinctive. The union raises hell because doing so is traditional. Without being judgmental or moralistic about it, I am simply pointing out the reality of the situation in the kind of unvarnished language you should have come to expect from me by now.

Only the most naive would try to deny that labor and management are adversaries. Which is the protagonist and which the antagonist depends on which side of the time clock you stand on. Since this is a book for and about managers, we must assume that the unions are the guys wearing the black hats. The executives are the good guys.

Should you study karate, you would learn in your first lesson to place both hands in front of you and bow to your opponent. This appears to be a gracious and courteous greeting. In reality, however, you are using your hands to protect your crotch so that this bastard won't catch you off guard. Your union relations should be approached with much the same wariness.

As an executive, you must look upon the union as a dangerous monkey wrench that has learned to throw itself into the works. To you it's a rare form of spontaneous sabotage. It must be thought of as sugar in the gas tank of business. (Too many metaphors? I think not. How do I know when you'll get the point?)

The struggle between the workers and the bosses is not, for the most part, open warfare, but rather a cold war. The altercation is not a win-or-lose affair, but rather a matter of maintaining the détente. Both sides want to have the mightier club, but neither side really wants to use it.

What would be gained if management were to destroy the work force? Nothing. The executives might have to go to work themselves. Most of us would admit not only an unwillingness but also a lack of competence if this were to happen. If the union members were to destroy their employers, for whom would they work? They might exult in biting the hand that feeds them from time to time, but not in chewing the entire creature to death.

This volume is not designed to tell union leaders or members what they should do. The author expects a hard enough time from the *New York Times Book Review,* the *Manchester Guardian,* the *Swanee Review, Sporting News, Commentary,* and "Sixty Minutes" without taking on the National Labor Relations Board. So I will content myself with giving beneficial advice to managers only.

The hit or miss philosophy for dealing with unions is a simple three-point program: (1) mollify, (2) collaborate, and (3) mollycoddle.

Mollify

You need workers. You expect from each of them eight hours of work per day. It's not to your benefit to have them working six hours and running back and forth to their union representatives for two hours. Therefore, you must look upon your workers as helpless infants who could begin bawling at any moment for the slightest of motives. In order to keep your corporation operating at a peak efficiency, you must keep your infants satisfied.

Collaborate

It is no sign of weakness to collaborate with the local union, any more than it is a sign of frailty for a parent to give in to a lachrymose offspring. Any parent who values a good night's rest will do everything possible to see that the child is fed, diapered, and comfortably cribbed before turning in. The parent wants to snore away without interruption, just as the manager wants business to continue without surcease. Translated, the parent's tender "Sleep well, my little loved one" really means, "I hope *I* can sleep well tonight, my little loudmouth." Anyone who derisively calls that parent a "collaborator" has never had to get up in the middle of the night for a three o'clock feeding.

Mollycoddle

Pamper your union members. Make sure their chairs are soft and free from annoying squeaks. Check to see that the office lighting is adequate. Keep the working conditions comfortable and the atmosphere pleasant. You're not giving in to them; you're giving in to yourself. Your place of business should be so proper that any tantrums from the labor force will only expose them to the world as the spoiled brats that they are.

However, therein lies a serious flaw in our allegory.

Unions do indeed have the emotions of an infant, but they harbor the evil intelligence of an adult. Even the most benign of mothers would be tempted to anger if her little one cried in the middle of the night not only for a dry diaper but also for a cost-of-living increase. Even the most patient of fathers would be upset if his infant woke up in the early hours of the morning crying not just for a warm bottle of milk but for 8 percent more warm milk than the kid down the street is getting.

In the interest of fairness, we must report also that even the most reasonable of infants woul have ample cause to cry if the father said that they have no milk, while the mother was in the bathroom taking a bath in the stuff.

Admittedly, our parable is imperfect. One major difference is that parents and children generally love one another. Labor and management fall slightly short of that. Faults exist on both sides, but this book can't attempt to solve all of them. After all, at $8.95 you have no right to expect me to terminate all of the world's problems. Nevertheless, our illustration does provide the clue as to how you, the manager, should treat your union members.

Let me not mislead you, though. Unions, no matter how well cared for, will cry. Your own children cry. It is to be expected. I remember when I was beginning a family. My mother would say to me, about her own grandchildren, "Let them cry a little. It's good for their lungs." Upper management will say the same thing to you.

Don't worry. The bigwigs at the corporate level will never let you spoil your workers. I would suppose that many of them are parents, but I suspect that their own children not only have to cry in the middle of the night, but also have to get up and carry a picket placard around the bed several times before these people will consent to the 3 A.M. feeding.

Of course, union officials are not saints either. They will call their strikes strategically, when they can do you the most harm. I would imagine as infants they made it a habit to cry during those times when the parents were trying to enjoy a quiet moment of marital bliss.

Despite all of this, you, as a devout hit or miss manager, should remain consistent in your demeanor toward the union. Be to them as the loving and caring parent is to the infant. Provide them with the necessities of corporate life. Keep them comfortable and contented. Treat them as kindly as you would your own children. But remember, also, they are not your own children, so don't let the little bastards get the best of you.

CHAPTER 21

The suggestion box

or
Anything your employees have
to say to you should be kept under
lock and key.

Present-day establishment management is doing very well, thank you. That's how they feel. They've got a great thing going, and the consumers are paying the prices, so they want no outside interference from anyone. Suggestion boxes are seen now only in cartoons in business magazines.

Only *Hit or Miss Management* has the audacity and the foresight to advocate suggestion boxes. One manager said to me early in my career, "If you put up a suggestion box, do you know what you will get? Exactly what you deserve." I disagree. It's a commendable practice, no matter how high or mighty you become, to listen to your employees. After all, they are entitled to their own stupid opinions.

Stop at a local bar some evening when Monday-night football is on television. Even if you don't like football, stop in anyway, because it's an education. As you view the game, one thing will become apparent to you: everyone in that bar can coach the team better than the person who is paid to do it.

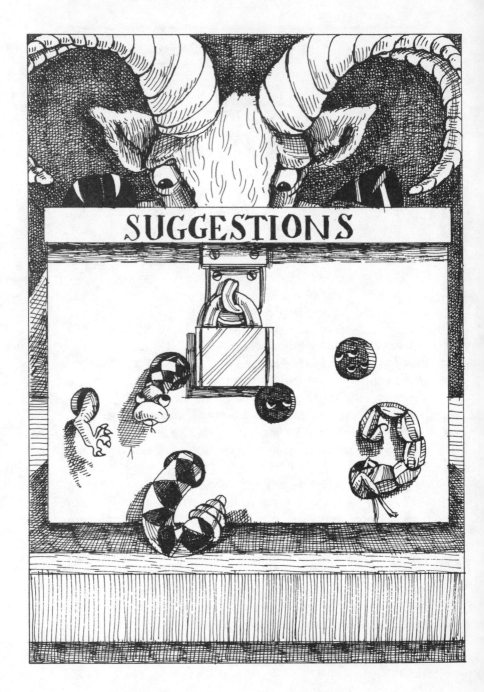

SUGGESTIONS

These civilians will find such obvious faults with the strategy that you'll be astounded the professionals failed to notice them.

The same applies in business. You are the chosen leader, the paid professional, but it is axiomatic that everyone in the organization who is lower in rank can run the business better than you. They inwardly sniggle at your blatant blunders. They gasp internally at your gross incompetence. Secretly they harbor the fantasy that, given the chance, they could turn this company around and become the executives of the year.

As long as your employees have these opinions, why not provide them with a platform to express them? An opinion that is kept inside can only smoulder and ferment into a grudge. The workers become angry at you for not utilizing their ideas, even though perhaps you didn't even know they had any. Their anger can escalate into near mutiny.

People like to speak up, so provide your employees with the platform that their psyches require. Give them an arena for their utopian ideologies. A story will illustrate my point.

A husband and wife were sleeping soundly. The woman awoke in the middle of the night. In trying to navigate through the midnight darkness to the bathroom, she stubbed her toe and let out a loud cry, which awakened her mate. He said, "What's going on?" She told of her painful collision with the bedpost. He said, "Oh, my poor dear, let me kiss it and make it better." He then began to kiss her foot, and in his ministrations he crept higher and higher until they were both overtaken by passion. In the afterglow of their lovemaking, the woman realized that she still had not visited the bathroom. She started again and banged the same toe on the same bedpost. The startled husband said, "What's the problem now?" She tearfully explained that she had injured her foot again. The satiated husband now said, "Well, watch where the hell you're going."

An impractical proposition is like lust. Once vented, it

loses its ardor. Once an idea is aired in flowery verbiage, it dissolves. The quickest way to quiet a passionate speaker is to ask him to chair a committee to study the problem. He'll disappear into the crowd like a shadow.

With your managerial duties, you don't have time to listen to all of your workers' ideas. You don't have the endurance to listen to all of them consecutively. You don't have the willpower to listen to all of them with a straight face. The suggestion box is your solution.

However, you should follow some commonsense safety measures in handling employee suggestions. The first thing you should do when opening the suggestion box is sort the suggestions from the candy wrappers, chewed-up gum, and other garbage that's dropped in there because your idealistic, ambitious workers are too lazy to walk to the nearest waste-basket.

Next, separate those suggestions that have to do with business operations from those that have to do with your physical being. Discard the personal proposals. Besides being useless, most of them are anatomically impossible. (Although once you get over the initial disgust, some of them might actually be fun to try.)

Never open a suggestion that is smoking, ticking, or rattling. And, of course, never open a suggestion that has breathing holes cut in the top.

Do read through the other suggestions at your leisure. You might even get one that you can use in your business. It happened to a guy in Shreveport once.

Even if you follow none of the other precepts of *Hit or Miss Management* (I can almost hear Drucker gloating), do install the suggestion box. Look at the wisdom of it. It's better to have your employees' ideas cooped up in a dark box than to have them roaming freely about. Besides, it keeps their propositions off the restroom walls.

CHAPTER 22

Physical and mental well-being

or

If you don't manage your own mind
and body, soon they'll both be in the same
lousy shape as your business.

You might say that this chapter is out of place in a management book, but try to keep in mind that you're not writing the book. I am, and I say it should be here. Remember that your first duty is to get your next R/P. Why get it if you're not going to be here to enjoy it?

All of our theories have been based on the natural, the organic, way of doing things. Taking care of yourself is natural.

In fact, merely becoming a *Hit or Miss Management* disciple will be beneficial to your health, because it is an easygoing philosophy. You try step one, and if it fails you proceed to step two complacent with the knowledge that step one's being wrong did no serious damage and step two's being right really does no appreciable good.

Hit or Miss Management by definition practically eliminates the stress factor. It is the stress factor that causes emotional disturbances, which in turn can cause physical ailments.

Dr. Thomas H. Holmes and his associate, Dr. Rahe,

from the University of Washington School of Medicine, have numerically rated the events in a person's life that can cause illness-producing stress. The scale they developed is shown in Table 1.

Although your author is not trained in medicine, I have devised the Perret Official Office Stress Scale. I have never allowed formal education or the lack thereof to stop me before. My scale is presented in Table 2.

TABLE 1
HOLMES AND RAHE'S STRESS RATING SCALE

EVENT	POINTS
Death of spouse	100
Divorce	73
Marital separation	65
Jail term	63
Death of close family member	63
Personal injury or illness	53
Marriage	50
Fired from work	47
Marital reconciliation	45
Retirement	45
Change in family member's health	44
Pregnancy	40
Sex difficulties	39
Addition to family	39
Business readjustment	39
Change in financial status	38
Death of close friend	37
Change to different line of work	36
Change in number of marital arguments	36
Mortgage or loan over $10,000	31
Foreclosure of mortgage or loan	30

EVENT	POINTS
Change in work responsibilities	29
Son or daughter leaving home	29
Trouble with in-laws	29
Outstanding personal achievement	28
Spouse begins or stops work	26
Starting or finishing school	26
Change in living conditions	25
Revision of personal habits	24
Trouble with boss	23
Change in work hours, conditions	20
Change in residence	20
Change in schools	20
Change in recreational habits	19
Change in church activities	19
Change in social activities	18
Mortgage or loan under $10,000	17
Change in sleeping habits	16
Change in number of family gatherings	15
Change in eating habits	15
Vacation	13
Christmas season	12
Minor violation of the law	11

TABLE 2

THE PERRET OFFICIAL OFFICE STRESS SCALE

EVENT	POINTS
Promotion of friend	100
Someone steals your desk copy of *Hit or Miss Management*	73

TABLE 2 *(Continued)*

EVENT	POINTS
Boss comes out of office and throws something at you	65
You learn nickname employees call you	63
Your desk chair given to superior	63
Third or more office collection that day	53
Boss wins World Series pool	50
Photocopier jams while you're copying dirty poem	47
Promotion of enemy	45
Second office collection that day	45
Rains during entire vacation	44
Everyone at meeting talks about party at boss's house you weren't invited to	40
No coffee comes out of vending machine	39
Coffee comes out of vending machine but no cup	39
No sugar comes out of vending machine	39
No milk comes out of vending machine	38
Coffee, milk, and sugar come out of vending machine perfectly, and then you taste it	37
First office collection that day	36
Promotion of anybody	36
You trip over bottom desk drawer you left open	31
People gathered around the watercooler point toward you and laugh	30
Somebody changed the hole locations in three-hole punch	29
Someone turns the thermostat up	29
Someone turns the thermostat down	29
Your briefcase falls open at meeting and your copy of *Playboy* falls out	28
At a presentation, your charts are out of order	26
At a presentation, your audience is out of order	26

EVENT	POINTS
You get a paper cut	25
You hand in your expense account	24
Point of your pencil keeps breaking off in sharpener	23
Someone spills coffee on desk	20
You're late for work	20
You're early for work	20
After washing hands you discover there are no towels in restroom dispenser	19
Instead of time card in your slot there is note that boss wants to see you	19
Secretary's skirt rides up	18
You pull paper clip out of your drawer and find someone clipped them all together	17
You look at clock at 4:10 and momentarily misread it as twenty after two	16
At quitting time, you're only one who can't jam into elevator	15
You read deductions on your paycheck stub	15
You receive a get-well card signed by everyone in office, but all the handwriting is the same	13
Picture on restroom wall resembles you	12
No office collection taken that day, but you're afraid there might be	11

I should stress, though—I'm sorry; I should *emphasize*—that this chart is listed here for the reference of those who, pitifully, have not yet embraced the *Hit or Miss Management* principles. With *Hit or Miss Management*, stress becomes as obsolete as green eyeshades in the accounting department.

CHAPTER 23

Sex in the office

or
How to handle those things
you can't take home in
your briefcase.

Those of you who turned to this chapter first — and you know who you are — should be ashamed of yourselves. This is a serious volume designed to revolutionize the management world. We all have a lot of important work to do, and you must read this book if you expect to be of any aid. There will be plenty of time for sex in the office after *Hit or Miss Management* is universally accepted. Now you should go back and read the book from the beginning.

I apologize to my more traditional readers for that outburst, but some decorum must be maintained. Now we can get on with the chapter.

Hit or Miss Management does recommend sex in the office as a revitalizer. A good friend of mine used to have his wife visit his private office every day after lunch. Which meant that he had to schedule his sex either before or after her visit.

Nonetheless, sex in the office is always effective. It's refreshing, revitalizing, and in the case of most executives only takes a minute or two.

I would not recommend any form of kinky sex at these matinees, though. What you do at home is between you,

166

your mate(s), and your conscience, but in the office, keep it straight. Sometimes the sound of the whip can be overheard, the whipped cream gets all over the files, and besides, you'd be surprised how many times you'll forget yourself and go to a staff meeting without taking the mask off.

Now, of course my fellow business authors totally neglect this subject. Well, they don't really neglect it. They just get *their* jollies with fiscal reports, financial statements, profit-and-loss charts, and other (for them) erotica.

That stuff doesn't titillate the hit or miss manager, however. Our philosophies have been gleaned from a study of nature. Sex is part of nature, and once again we can draw wisdom from our furry, feathered, and scaled friends.

Animals make no distinction between sex and work. Have you ever noticed beavers building a dam? They're all naked. That's why they build the dam. They watch one another cavorting about the forest in the nude. They watch their coworkers pounding mud with those attractive tails, and, to be quite frank, it gets them a little horny.

They build the dam so they can have a little privacy. Sure, their tails are sort of tired and aching at the end of the dam workday, but they're not so weary that they can't get it on. Not even a beaver, however, wants to get it on in front of the leers of the local water moccasins or an uncouth muskrat.

Because they're horny, they build the dam, and the building of the dam gets them horny. It's the organic cycle of nature.

In the animal kingdom, work and sex are quite naturally interrelated. Animals work for food, shelter, and sex. Only humans work for food, shelter, and clothing. Animals don't need clothes because they're not embarrassed by sex.

That's another reason why we humans become lazy. Our sex has become separated from our work. If, like the beaver, when we finished a project, we were rewarded with the favors of one of our working companions, you would see output production that would knock your eyes out. Our friend Drucker would see results not even he could manage.

It is the natural way. Have you ever heard of an impotent beaver? Do you think he climbs into his comfortable nest at night and says to his wife, "Naw, I can't tonight, dear. I gotta build a dam in the morning, and this dam could be very important to my career?"

They all work together, and they all make whoopee together (at more or less the same time, I mean). That again is better than our system. No beaver has ever fooled around with another beaver while her husband was on the night shift.

Your author says: To be happy in the business world, act like an animal. Enjoy sex with your work and work with your sex.

Now I'm not advocating nudity at work . . . yet. Let's at least wait until we get the air-conditioning wars settled. But, as in the case of our tiny creature friends, sex in the office can be an incentive. Animals work hard to enjoy sex. You've never seen a bachelor bird building a nest. Why do all that work if you're not going to score?

Likewise, an executive should work hard to get a private office because sex is easier to enjoy there than, say, in the cafeteria.

Is this chapter controversial? Certainly. Is it important to the *Hit or Miss* movement? Absolutely. This one point will probably win more converts than the rest of the book put together.

Yes, when *Hit or Miss Management* becomes universally adopted, sex in the office will be commonplace, natural, and free of shame.

That's all the more reason why you should go back and reread the previous chapter on your physical well-being. When that glorious day arrives, you'd better be in shape for it.

CHAPTER 24

Travel tips

or

In your corporate headquarters,
you may be Vice President in charge of
Residential Sales and General Manager of
East Coast Operations with responsibility
for new business research and acquisition,
but on an airplane, you're a passenger.

Every so often, the executive must leave his lair. Periodically, like a baby sparrow, he is nudged from his nest by upper management and must wing away to visit satellite offices, learn more about his trade at seminars, or try to interest another buyer in the company's services. It's almost like birth: it's wonderfully exciting because you burst into a new world of infinite mystery and adventure, but you must leave the secure sanctuary where you literally swim in solace and contentment.

The outside world is alien to the executive because it strips him in one swipe of his dominion. On foreign ground, he lords it over no one, and he has no orders from upstairs to rely on. As a private citizen he is on his own, and it's terrifying.

It's not uncommon for defectors from dictatorial nations to return to the nation they rejected after tasting freedom. Independence is too much of a burden on them. They rel-

ish the inflexible domination of the state because it removes the responsibility of free choice.

A similar discomfort gnaws at the entrails of the traveling executive. He tries to seem self-assured, but inwardly he longs to be back in his cozy office where the rules are known. He wants once again to be a prisoner behind the pin-stripe curtain.

Our migrating executive is offended by anyone in the outside world who dares to be his peer, and he is absolutely incensed at any unfortunate who in any small way considers himself (heaven forbid) a superior. He rails at restaurant hostesses who presume to tell him where to sit. He castigates hotel clerks who give him rooms beneath his stature. He vituperates cabbies who arrogantly suggest an economic shortcut. He wants no one to tell him where to go (although everyone would like to).

The traveling executive is an ogre. Why? Because he has read and believed all that pap that has been fed to him by my confreres, the establishment management writers. They have fostered the impression that an executive is a somebody. *Hit or Miss Management*, on the other hand, is of the opinion that an executive is an anybody.

Nowhere is the difference between today's establishment manager and the hit or miss manager more apparent than when you get the two out of their lairs.

The establishment managers must constantly prove themselves. They are like captured gorillas in the zoo, always beating their chests in a ferocious display of superiority. In the wild, gorillas hang around together and are good family animals, playfully romping and solicitously caring for their young. Basically, they're nice creatures, but put them in a cage with strange people passing before them, and all they think about is showing how powerful they are. Traveling establishment executives are in that same cage.

The *Hit or Miss* manager can sit back and enjoy his journey. He knows that even in his office he's no big deal, so why try to prove it to strangers?

Defeat this apelike tendency in yourself. Cherish and enjoy your travel time. It's the one chance you get to be paid by the company simply to be a human being. And be just that—a human being boarding an aircraft for a flight to somewhere with a bunch of other human beings. It's nice. You'll have plenty of time to act like an imbecilic ape once you get back to your office.

Although I abhor anything that smacks of Druckerism, I must say that *Hit or Miss Management* travel behavior gets results. It is far more effective than the establishment manager's demeanor.

Let's picture two executives on a flight to Chicago. One is your standard manager, the other is your author. Both of us were pressed for time and had to be in Chicago. Compare the methods and the effects of the two.

SETTING: A DC-10 aircraft at the terminal of Philadelphia's International Airport. A stewardess is helping the passengers board.

STEWARDESS. *(as our establishment executive enters)* May I see your boarding pass, sir?

HIM. I know where my seat is. I've flown this airline for over 100,000 miles this year, and I demand the same seat each time.

STEWARDESS. *(looking at the pass)* That's seat 7c, sir.

HIM. You're damn right it is. It's an aisle seat on the nonsunny side of the aircraft, and you'd better not put any noisy chatterboxes next to me. I don't have any time for small talk because I have a report to get ready before we touch down in Chicago.

STEWARDESS. You're holding up the people behind you, sir.

HIM. You can tell all those people behind me that I fly over

100,000 miles a year on this airline, and if they don't like being held up, I'll just switch to another airline without giving it a second thought.

(This gentleman reluctantly moved to his assigned—I beg your pardon, demanded—seat, and the stewardess checked in the other passengers without incident. Later, as we prepared for takeoff, Gorilla man called the stewardess over.)

HIM. Hey.

STEWARDESS. Are you calling me, sir?

HIM. What time are we due in Chicago?

STEWARDESS. Our arrival time is 3:15, sir.

HIM. That's no good.

STEWARDESS. But your ticket is for Chicago, isn't it, sir?

HIM. Don't you think after flying 100,000 miles a year on this airline that I know how to read a ticket? I know we're going to Chicago, but I have to get there by 3:00—no later.

STEWARDESS. Sir, our scheduled time has always been 3:15, and we . . .

HIM. Come here. . . . Listen to me, honey.

STEWARDESS. Sir, take your hand off of my bottom.

HIM. Just give this card to the pilot. *(He gives her one of his embossed business cards.)* Tell him that I want to be in Chicago by three sharp. If he wants to keep his job with this airline, he'd damn well better make it by that time. I have a director's meeting to get to, and no smart-ass pilot is going to make me late for it.

STEWARDESS. Sir, I'll gladly tell him all about you.

(She starts toward the cockpit.)

HIM. Wait a minute. *(taking a pen out of his pocket and grabbing the card back from her)* Let me write on here how many thousands of miles a year I travel with this airline.

(He writes and hands the card back. The stewardess goes up into the cockpit in a huff.)

CAPTAIN. Hey, what's the matter, Wanda?

STEWARDESS. Captain, get your hand off my bottom.

CAPTAIN. Wow, what's wrong with you?

STEWARDESS. I got this jerk out there who says if you don't get us to Chicago by three, he's going to have you fired.

CAPTAIN. Goddamn it, who is it this time?

STEWARDESS. Here's his card.

CAPTAIN. You tell that bastard what he can do with his card and also tell him that when we land in Chicago I will personally do the same thing with his luggage . . . and I hope he's carrying a set of golf clubs.

That's the end of scene one. But now scene two features the same stewardess and the father of *Hit or Miss Management,* your humble author.

ME. *(to the annoyed stewardess, who has just left the cockpit)* Excuse me, Miss?

STEWARDESS. What?

ME. Oh, I'm sorry. If you're too busy I can speak with you later.

STEWARDESS. No, that's all right. May I help you?

ME. I was just wondering what our estimated arrival time for Chicago was.

STEWARDESS. Don't tell me . . . you're a businessman, you've traveled over 100,000 miles with this airline, and you're late for a board meeting.

ME. Well, yes, all of that is true, but I'm not just a businessman, I'm a *Hit or Miss* manager.

STEWARDESS. Well, it's about time I got one of those. I generally get the establishment kind, you know.

ME. Oh, I'm sorry, dear. Then I won't bother you with my problems.

STEWARDESS. No, it's no bother. I'd enjoy talking to you. What can I do for you?

ME. Just tell the captain, when he's not busy, that I would appreciate being in Chicago by three o'clock, and if he can do it I would be pleased to buy him a bottle of champagne.

STEWARDESS. I'll tell him right away, sir.

(She exits into the cockpit.)

STEWARDESS. Excuse me, captain, but one of our passengers said he'd give you a bottle of champagne if you could shave fifteen minutes off the flying time.

CAPTAIN. Champagne! No kidding. Prepare for takeoff. Contact.

COPILOT. But captain, they're still loading baggage on board.

CAPTAIN. Forget the luggage, you fool. We're talking champagne!

COCAPTAIN. Yes, sir.

NAVIGATOR. Sir?

CAPTAIN. What is it, navigator?

NAVIGATOR. If you promise to cut me in on some of that bubbly, sir, I know a shortcut to Chicago.

CAPTAIN. You've got it. Let's go.

COCAPTAIN. We don't have clearance from the tower, sir.

CAPTAIN. Damn the tower. We're going for it.

(The engines roar, and the plane begins its takeoff. As the plane is climbing, the pilot turns to his copilot.)

CAPTAIN. Hennessey?

COPILOT. Yes, sir?

CAPTAIN. Get that first businessman's card from Wanda, then radio ahead to Chicago. Have them send that jackass's luggage to Cleveland.

COPILOT. *(gleefully)* Roger, sir.

CHAPTER 25

Expense accounts

or
You can get blood from a rock,
if the rock doesn't look too closely.

The talk of travel begets the talk of expense accounts. Our hit or miss management philosophy says that you really shouldn't agonize over anything, because in the long run nothing matters anyway. However, all of that was when I was talking about THEIR money. With expense accounts I'm talking about MY money. Some agonizing is definitely in order here.

My first respect for expense accounts came when I was a youngster of about nine or ten. My friend and I were going to a baseball game in Schibe Park in Philadelphia. I was given two bucks to spend, so Jimmy's mother also gave him two big ones for spending money. We went to the game and had a great old time. When we got home, Jimmy's mother asked for change, and he had none to offer. She beat the living hell out of him, right in front of me . . . and I had no change to give my mother, either.

It was there, as Jimmy was squealing to the sting of the strap, that I concluded that spending money was given, not to spend, but rather to save as emergency funding, and it was to be returned or precisely accounted for.

It was at exactly the same time that the devious machinations of my mind deduced that in order to keep the spending money, some prevarications must be offered instead of change.

The following is a reproduction of my first recorded expense account.

Detailed expenses for
Going to the Ball Game,
1) car fare (2 + from)   18¢
2) car fare (again)   18¢
3) admission to game   50¢
4) Lunch (1 hot dog w/   — 35¢
   everything - 1 coke small
5) Tip for hot dog vender 25¢
6) ransom for Jimmy 54 ¢

total = $2.00
charge to mom - none

signed your loving son,
                GENE

My mother gave me a tanning that surpassed Jimmy's punitive thrashing. She didn't buy the story about us getting lost and having to pay double carfare (item 2) any more than she bought the story about Jimmy getting kidnapped and me rescuing him (item 6). But don't let this frighten you. My mom was smarter than any corporation existing today.

Now I would not condone nor do I endorse cheating on your expense account. It is simply a vehicle whereby you are to be reimbursed by the corporation for expenditures validly incurred by you in your journey. It's not designed to help you make a profit.

However, there are ways of employing this document to pay for some expenses that are not normally allowed by the accounting department. For instance, every executive in the world lists an $8.00 expense for cab fare to the airport. This is generally accepted by the company, but I'd like to see how it is accepted by the businessman's wife who had to get up that morning in her slippers and robe to drive him to the terminal in time for his flight. She probably didn't even get a tip.

And every doorman, redcap, and waiter and waitress in the universe longs for the day when he or she will encounter an executive who is as big a tipper as he claims to be on his expense report.

I repeat that I don't recommend this as a form of cheating . . . but I don't really condemn it, either. It's all a matter of attitude. In filling out the reimbursement form, you must do it with the frame of mind that the company is saying to you, "Enjoy a safe and pleasant trip, and have a couple of drinks on me."

CHAPTER 26

Head rolling time

or
All good things must come to an end.
Every once in a while, you're a good thing.

If anything, *Hit or Miss Management* is realistic. Throughout this book we have emphasized that management is not important. Managers can do no good, but if they are careful they can also cause no harm. They're like that middle pedal on a piano. No one knows what it does or why it is there, but it is traditional, and it does separate the other two pedals.

Being in management sure as hell beats being a bomb defuser. One mistake there, and you're through. Make a mistake in management, though, and nobody notices. If it's a tremendously drastic mistake, they just raise prices.

So we managers have it pretty good. However, like all good things, it must come to an end. Very few people in high executive slots live out their careers working for the same company. Sooner or later this job of yours will probably come to an end. In fact, if you follow the precepts laid down in *Hit or Miss Management*, I can almost guarantee it.

For example, my head has rolled so often, I've developed retractable ears. In each instance it was so that a better person could replace me. At least, that was the company line.

It was impossible to fight, so I simply tested their story. I had nothing else to do anyway.

I waited six months. This would give the replacement a fair opportunity to start having an effect on the company. Then I went out and bought one of the corporation's products, and, sure enough, it still didn't work. I bought a table radio, and the tuning knob fell off. It could have done that with me at the helm.

You can't name one instance in which replacing someone at the management level improved the company's products or services in any way. This is simply further proof that management makes no difference. Head rolling, head chopping, bloodletting, whatever—none of these will have any effect on the company. Then why do they do it? It could be as simple as this: the top management just wants to get some people into their meetings who haven't heard their jokes yet.

However, it will have an effect on you personally. You will have to find new worlds to conquer, other roads to travel, different watercooler lines to stand in.

It's traumatic for you to be laid off. Now you have to make some decisions, and you have no committees to help you or to blame for mistakes.

Therefore, it is to your benefit to learn early if the ax will fall on you or not. There are some telltale signs that you should look for. Believe me, I know them well because I've seen them all.

Yes, I, your author, the father of *Hit or Miss Management*, have been through sundry severing encounters. I've been mature enough throughout my career to realize that I do no real good for any of my employers, but, on the other hand, I do them no lasting harm either. Therefore, when I see the ominous signs of termination approaching, I fight like a son of a bitch.

You should, too. What the hell. We know the new person will be no better than you were, so why not collect your paycheck for a few weeks longer?

The best way I can educate you in the methods of postponing or avoiding, if possible, the corporate ax is to recount for you the drama of my most recent separation.

SETTING: The vice-president's office. I am ushered in by his secretary.

ME. Hi, boss. You sent for me. What is it? Have you got a problem?

BOSS. Yes, I do. A very big problem.

ME. Well, just name it, boss, and I'll get right on it in my usual way.

BOSS. Gene Perret.

ME. Right. That's me, here at your beck and call. Now name the problem.

BOSS. Gene Perret.

ME. Huh?

BOSS. You, clunkhead, you're the problem.

ME. Could you be a little more specific, sir? I'm not sure I understand.

BOSS. I don't think you've understood anything since the day you arrived here.

ME. Sir, I beg to differ with you, but I think I understand more than you think.

BOSS. You don't understand shit.

ME. Now, sir, I think the other managers are a bit upset because I subscribe to a different philosophy than most of them.

BOSS. Your philosophy is different from most sane people's.

ME. Thank you, sir.

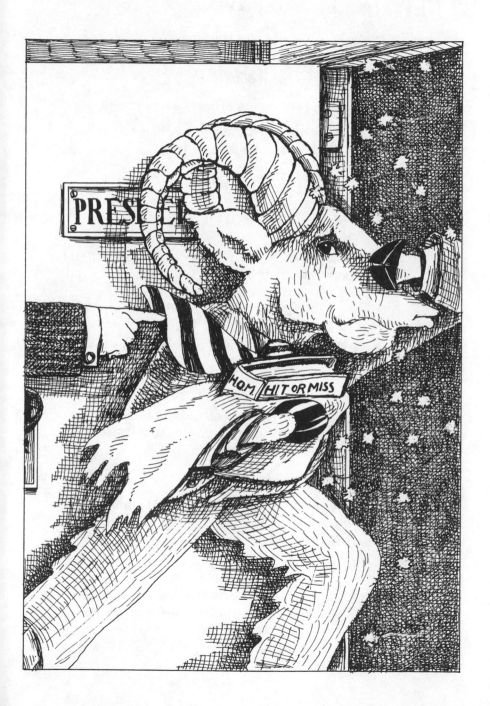

BOSS. You just don't fit into this organization. When I want a budget report from you, I get a story about how your brother used to buy copybooks.

ME. Now, sir, I try . . .

BOSS. When I ask who you're going to hire, I get a story about some cock-eyed, knock-kneed goat.

ME. That's a ram, sir.

BOSS. That's a pain in the ass, Perret.

ME. The purpose of that . . .

BOSS. I've seen some of the stupid reports you've written. I want a report from my production manager, and I wind up with a cockamamie Mother Goose story.

ME. What that was meant to convey . . .

BOSS. I ask you to attend a meeting and you tell me that ants don't have meetings.

ME. They don't, sir.

BOSS. Well, I don't go to picnics and walk all over other people's food, either. I ask how you make a decision, you tell me about a cheetah catching a zebra.

ME. They've never caught a bad one, sir.

BOSS. Well, I sure did. I plead with you to give your employees our company policy, and you tell me how you took some girl's bra off in the back of a car.

ME. You can learn from everything, sir.

BOSS. I ask you about cutting costs, you tell me about toys. I'm worried about union problems, you're giving lessons on three o'clock baby feedings. I ask you to take a business trip, and I can't get any of the airlines to accept you as a passenger.

ME. That last one has me puzzled, sir.

BOSS. And I saw your last expense account. We have no record of any friend of yours being kidnapped.

ME. I can explain that, sir.

BOSS. Let *me* explain something to *you*, Perret. Go down to your office and take down those kids' pictures, which I know you didn't draw yourself, take your phony red telephone, pack up all that other crap, and get your ass out of here.

(I recognized this as one of the signs of imminent termination, so I fight to postpone it.)

ME. But sir, what will I do?

BOSS. Why don't you become one of those cock-eyed, knock-kneed goats you're always talking about. I think you could excel at that sort of work.

ME. May I call the hospital to tell my mother not to have the operation?

BOSS. Don't touch that phone, you nitwit. Everything you've touched around here has cost me money.

ME. This is going to be very hard on my children. Especially the little one, who likes you so much.

BOSS. The little crippled one that you nicknamed Tiny Tim?

ME. How did you know, sir?

BOSS. I called and talked to the last vice-president who fired you.

(My intuitions tell me that there will be no postponing this hatchet job. This vice-president is one tough cookie. I decide to get nasty.)

ME. Sir, I've got a good mind to quit.

BOSS. Holy sweetheart, you are the dumbest human being I ever met.

ME. And you, sir, are a present-day establishment manager for whom I have no respect.

BOSS. Just get the hell out.

ME. Don't beat around the bush with me, sir. I know when I'm being fired. I've been through it before.

BOSS. I'll bet you have.

ME. I was fired Tuesday of this week. Friday of last week. The Tuesday before. Twice on the Friday before that. And many, many times before that, so don't try to treat me as if I were born yesterday.

BOSS. I just wish to hell you were *fired* yesterday.

ME. Sir, you leave me no alternative but to retire from this establishment and to work for your competitors.

BOSS. Perret, if you did that, I'd be eternally grateful.

ME. Don't mention it, sir.

BOSS. In fact . . . *(His eyes light up with glee.)* . . . why don't you do something else for my competitors? Why don't you write that stupid book on management you've always talked about?

Well, to make a long story short . . . I did.

Acknowledgments II

The author, the father of *Hit or Miss Management,* wishes to thank his confreres in the field of managerial literature, without whose observations he would have been completely lost. I only hope that all of these fine authors will buy a copy of *Hit or Miss Management,* and then have two of their friends buy copies, and then each of them have two of *their* friends buy copies, and so on and so on. . . .